Eyewitness
EXPLORER

Shoot and bark from *cinchona* plant from which quinine is obtained

Sealskin hood and mitten from Arctic expedition 1875–76

Map showing Phoenicia on the eastern coast of the Mediterranean

Incan cup

Captain Meriwether Lewis, American explorer

Spanish doubloons made from South American gold

Butterfly brought back from Australia by Joseph Banks

Eyewitness
EXPLORER

Written by
RUPERT MATTHEWS

Lodestone—naturally magnetic iron oxide—used by early explorers when navigating at sea

Charles Darwin's compass

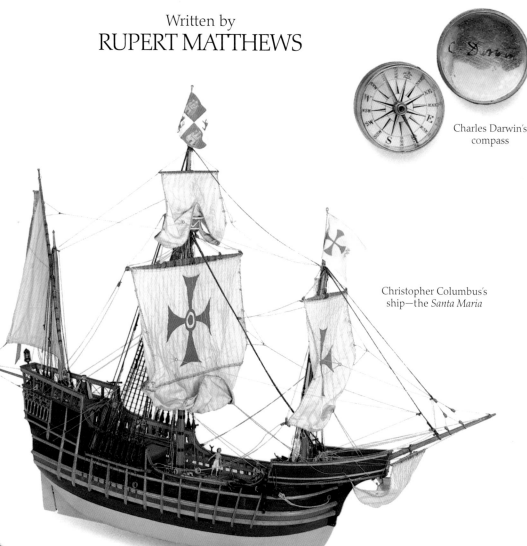
Christopher Columbus's ship—the *Santa Maria*

Cloves were brought back aboard the first ship to sail around the world

Indian wooden
mask presented to
Charles Wilkes and
Meriwether Lewis

LONDON, NEW YORK,
MELBOURNE, MUNICH, and DELHI

Project editor Linda Martin
Art editor Alison Anholt-White
Senior editor Helen Parker
Senior art editor Julia Harris
Production Louise Barratt
Picture research Kathy Lockley
Special photography
James Stevenson, Tina Chambers,
Keith Percival, Barrie Cash of
the National Maritime Museum, London; Alan Hills, Ivor Curzlake,
Philip Nicholls and Chas Howson of the British Museum, London

REVISED EDITION

Revised by Steve Setford

DK INDIA
Project editor Shatarupa Chaudhuri
Project art editor Honlung Zach Ragui
Editor Priyanka Kharbanda
Senior art editor Govind Mittal
Managing editor Saloni Talwar
Managing art editor Romi Chakraborty
DTP designer Tarun Sharma
Picture researcher Sumedha Chopra

DK UK

Senior editors Rob Houston, Caroline Stamps
Senior art editor Philip Letsu
Production editor Adam Stoneham
Production controller Gemma Sharpe
Publisher Andrew Macintyre

DK US

US editor Margaret Parrish
Editorial director Nancy Ellwood

This revised edition published in the United States in 2012
by DK Publishing, 375 Hudson Street, New York, New York 10014
First published in the United States in 1991

10 9 8 7 6 5 4 3 2 1
001–183521– September/12

Viking gold rings
found in Ireland

Banjo taken
on Ernest
Shackleton's
Antarctic
expedition

DK books are available at special discounts when purchased in
bulk for sales promotions, premiums, fundraising, or educational use.
For details, contact: DK Publishing Special Markets, 375 Hudson Street,
New York, New York 10014
SpecialSales@dk.com

A catalog record for this book is available from
the Library of Congress.

ISBN: 978-0-7566-9825-6
ISBN: 978-0-7566-9826-3 (Library binding)

Color reproduction by Colourscan, Singapore
Printed in China by Toppan Co., (Shenzhen) Ltd.

Inuit bone
knives

Discover more at
www.dk.com

Contents

Henry Stanley's hat

6
Early explorers
8
Egyptian expeditions
10
Imperial expansion
12
Viking voyages
14
Polynesian settlers
16
The Silk Road
18
Arab adventurers
20
The Age of Exploration
22
The New World
24
Around the world
26
Life at sea
28
Tricks of the trade
30
Gold and the gospel
34
The Great South Sea
36
The Endeavour
38
Across Australia
40
The Northwest Passage
42
North America explored

46
The unknown continent
48
Naturalist explorers
52
The North Pole
54
The South Pole
56
Pioneers of the air
58
Into outer space
60
Exploring the deep
62
Exploration routes
64
Did you know?
66
Timeline of exploration
68
Find out more
70
Glossary
72
Index

Early explorers

SIX THOUSAND YEARS AGO, people knew little of what existed more than a few days' journey away from their own homes. Because they could grow all their own food and make everything they needed, they had no need to travel far. However, as civilization developed, so did the idea of trading goods with other countries. One of the earliest peoples to begin trading were the Phoenicians, who lived in cities on the Mediterranean coast of what is now Israel and Lebanon. The Phoenicians were expert shipbuilders and were able to sail great distances. They also realized that they could make money by trading. Between about 1100 BCE and 700 BCE, Phoenician ships explored the entire Mediterranean, searching for new markets and establishing colonies. They even sailed through the Strait of Gibraltar to the Atlantic, and reached Britain and West Africa.

GLASS BEADS
Phoenician craftsmen were expert glassworkers and were able to produce intricate pieces that were then sold abroad. This necklace was found in a tomb on the site of the ancient city of Tharros in Sardinia.

Demon head

Disk representing the world

Carthaginian coin from Spain

Copper coin from Cádiz

EARLY MAP
This clay tablet was found in Iraq and shows the earliest-known map of the world. The world is surrounded by an ever-flowing stream, the Bitter River.

COINS
Early Phoenician merchants "swapped" goods, but later traders used coins—pieces of metal stamped to show their origin.

Silver coin from Carthage

Burial urn

Underground cellars

Phoenician inscription

BURIAL URN
This urn, found in Carthage, North Africa (near present-day Tunis), contains the bones of a child. Carthage was the main trading center for all Phoenician colonies. It was the custom there to sacrifice children to gods and goddesses; the bones were then buried in pottery burial urns in underground cellars.

BROKEN POTTERY
This piece of broken pottery is inscribed in Phoenician with the name of the powerful and beautiful goddess Astarte. It was found on the island of Malta, which lay on several shipping routes. Malta was colonized by the Phoenicians as a trading center.

118537

Star
Crescent and disk

Lotus flower

Monkey

JASPER SEAL
Ornamental seals were favorite items throughout the Mediterranean. High-quality pieces like this were carved by Phoenician craftsmen from jasper mined in Sardinia and shipped elsewhere for sale.

FOOD POWER
The Phoenicians shipped grain from Spain to many cities. Their control of the food supply made the Phoenicians extremely powerful.

BRONZE BOWL
Phoenician trade helped to spread culture and ideas. Made by a Phoenician metalsmith in about 750 BCE, this bronze bowl is decorated with motifs used by the Egyptians. It was later exported to the Assyrian Empire, in modern Iraq.

COPPER CARRIER
This figure of a Phoenician merchant was found in Cyprus. He is carrying copper, which the Phoenicians collected from Cyprus to trade elsewhere.

WESTWARD BOUND
The Phoenicians dominated trade and exploration in the Mediterranean for several hundred years. As you can see from this map, they sailed westward from their homeland in the Middle East, finding new peoples with whom to trade goods.

DEMON MASK
It is thought that this terra-cotta mask was intended to frighten away evil spirits. It may represent a demon and was found in the tomb of a Phoenician on the island of Sardinia in the Mediterranean.

BALAWAT GATES *below*
This bronze plaque from a pair of gates was found at Balawat in Iraq. It depicts Phoenician officials leaving Tyre. The king and queen (left) watch them as they set sail.

Silver coin from Sidon showing a Phoenician galley

Gates of Tyre

Loaded ships

Cargo being unloaded

Egyptian expeditions

THE WORLD'S EARLIEST CIVILIZATIONS, of which Egypt was one, developed in the rich lands of the Middle East. By 3000 BCE, Egypt had become a state, and numerous towns and cities sprang up in the fertile valley of the Nile River. According to Egyptian belief—as taught by the priests—the world was flat and rectangular; the heavens were supported by four massive pillars at each corner of the Earth, beyond which lay the Ocean—"a vast, endless stretch of ever-flowing water." At first, the Egyptians stayed in the Nile Valley, but they soon began traveling farther afield in search of new peoples to trade with. One of the most famous Egyptian voyages was made to Punt at the command of Queen Hatshepsut (see below). Despite this expedition, Egyptian priests simply declared that the sky supports were farther away than they thought!

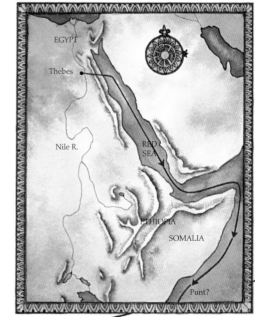

REED BOATS
Before the Egyptians found cedar wood for building oceangoing boats, sailing was restricted to the Nile River. Nile boats were made from reeds lashed together to form a slightly concave (inward-curving) structure.

ROYAL CARTOUCHE
A cartouche is an oval shape in which characters representing a sovereign's names are written. This is the cartouche of Queen Hatshepsut.

Faience

Lapis lazuli

BEETLE RINGS
Egyptian rings were often made with a stone in the shape of a scarab beetle. These scarab rings carry the cartouche of Queen Hatshepsut and belonged to her officials. They are made of gold, faience (glazed ceramic), and lapis lazuli that was imported from other lands.

QUEEN HATSHEPSUT
Around 1490 BCE, Queen Hatshepsut sent a fleet of ships southward through the Red Sea, and possibly as far as the Indian Ocean. The expedition found a country called Punt (probably modern-day Somalia, East Africa), where they were delighted to find ivory, ebony, and myrrh trees.

WOODEN SHIP *below*
After about 2700 BCE, the Egyptians began building wooden sailing ships capable of sea voyages. These ships sailed along the Mediterranean coasts to trade with nearby countries.

Bow (front of ship)

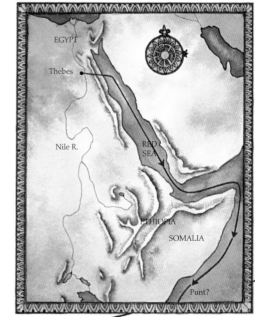

Map showing the route the Egyptians took to Punt

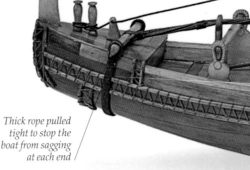

PRETTY FACES
Egyptian nobility wore large amounts of makeup, which they kept in containers such as this. Merchants explored many areas of North Africa and western Asia in the search for cosmetic ingredients.

Thick rope pulled tight to stop the boat from sagging at each end

Blue faience

Ivory inlay

Ebony

MYRRH
Myrrh was
a vital part
of Egyptian
religious ceremonies.
Egyptian explorers
brought back myrrh
and frankincense
from Punt. As well as
the gum resin, they
also carried back
myrrh trees to plant
in front of Queen
Hatshepsut's temple.

Myrrh gum resin

GEM OF A BOX
This Egyptian box is
made of ebony wood
with an ivory inlay,
and may well have been
used for storing jewelry. Both
ebony and ivory were among the
precious cargo that the Egyptian
explorers brought back from Punt.

This copy of a tomb
painting shows
Egyptians making
piles of incense

Pellets
burned here

Container for
pellets of incense

BRONZE BURNER
Incense, such as myrrh and frankincense, was
burned at all Egyptian religious ceremonies and
was very valuable. This bronze incense burner
has a falcon head and may have been sacred
to the sky god Horus.

Falcon head

Cinnamon sticks

Stern (back
of ship)

Mast

SAUCY SPICES
Cinnamon spice was
frequently used in cooking by rich Egyptians. It
came from the coast of India, from where it was
shipped by Arabs to Arabia (pp. 18–19) for sale
to Egyptian merchants.

Steering oars

STRONG CEDAR
Seagoing ships such as the
one on the left were built from
cedar wood that the Egyptians
brought back from Lebanon.

Imperial expansion

T HE MEDITERRANEAN WAS dominated by two great empires during the period between about 350 BCE and 500 CE. Alexander the Great, king of Macedonia (now part of northern Greece), conquered a vast empire that stretched from Greece to Egypt to India. The later Roman Empire was even larger, reaching from northern Britain to the Sahara desert in Africa, and from the Black Sea to the Atlantic Ocean. It was a time of great exploration and expansion, both on land and at sea. Alexander sent ambassadors to the distant lands of northern India to establish contacts. Roman emperors sent many expeditions both into Europe and south into Africa. Much exploration, however, was undertaken by private merchants and travelers; some evidence of their activities can be seen on these pages. One Greek merchant is said to have sailed to Iceland in search of new lands, while Romans traded with the wandering nomad peoples of Central Asia.

JASON AND THE ARGONAUTS
The Ancient Greek legends of Jason—a brave sailor who voyaged to many distant countries—were almost certainly romanticized accounts of real Greek journeys of exploration.

Alexander sent peacocks from India to Greece

THE HAWK
This gold Greek brooch was found in Ephesus, an Ancient Greek city just south of present-day Izmir in Turkey.

TRADING SOUTH
This small stone baboon was found on the site of Naucratis, a Greek colony in the Nile delta. The colony was founded in about 540 BCE by Greek merchants who traded for spices from Arabia and ivory from Africa.

BLACK SEA

MACEDONIA

Cyzicus

GREECE TURKEY

Tigris River

CASPIAN SEA

Oxus River

MEDITERRANEAN SEA

Byblos
Sidon
Tyre

Babylon

PERSIA

AFRICA Alexandria

Euphrates River

Sahara Desert

EGYPT
Memphis
Nile River

ARABIA

This map shows Alexander's route

PERSIAN GULF

PAKISTAN

Indus River INDIA

ALEXANDER THE GREAT
In 334 BCE, Alexander, king of Macedonia, led a Greek army into the great Persian Empire. By 327 BCE, he had captured an area that stretched from Egypt in the west to the Indus River, Pakistan in the east. The following year, he conquered parts of northern India before returning to Persia. His vast empire allowed Greek merchants and travelers to penetrate deep into Asia.

This coin shows Alexander attacking an Indian king

PERILS OF THE JOURNEY
The design on this Greek drinking cup shows a merchant vessel being pursued by a pirate ship. Merchants returning from distant lands with rich cargoes made easy prey.

FRUITS OF THE SEA
This Greek plate was made in Apulia, a Greek settlement in southern Italy. Fishing was an important industry there; dried fish was traded by Greek merchants throughout the Mediterranean.

Roman ships often had a carved swan's head at the stern

ROMAN RUINS
The ruined Roman city of Timgad, in Algeria, North Africa, would once have been filled by merchants trading with the desert nomads for gold, ivory, and slaves from lands south of the Sahara Desert.

The twins Romulus and Remus, said to have founded Rome

Steering oar

ROMAN MERCHANT SHIP
Merchant ships of the Roman Empire had two masts and a wide cargo hold. Such ships could not sail against the wind and were only put to sea when the wind was favorable. These ships brought back wild animals from Africa to fight Roman gladiators, and they also carried rich cargoes of gems, spices, and silk from Asia (pp. 16–17).

Roman glass bowl

TRADING EXPLORERS
The Roman silver cup on the right was found in Britain and is thought to have been imported by Roman traders—the first Romans other than Caesar's soldiers to explore Britain. The glass bowl on the left was found in the eastern Mediterranean.

Indian coin

Arabian coin

Roman silver cup

FOREIGN IMITATIONS
Roman influence spread far beyond the Empire's frontiers. These coins carry Roman designs, but were actually minted in Arabia and India.

CAESAR IN FRANCE
This Roman coin was made in the Roman colony of Vienne, southern France, around 36 BCE. The letters "CI V" stand for "Colonia Julia Viennensis," the "Colony of Julius Caesar at Vienne."

Prow of Roman galley

Viking voyages

Europe was seldom free from the menace of ruthless Viking raiders during the early Middle Ages. From the 8th to the 12th century, boatloads of Vikings left their Scandinavian homeland on voyages of exploration—plundering and pillaging the unfortunate communities they found in Britain and the Mediterranean. The motives for these journeys were varied. Some Vikings were interested only in stealing treasure and capturing slaves. But others were prompted to search for new lands across the Atlantic where they could settle, since farming land in Scandinavia was scarce. The Swedish Vikings, who were mainly traders, set their sights on the lands of Eastern Europe and Asia, with a view to developing new trading markets. After about 1200, the Vikings became more settled and ceased their long voyages of discovery.

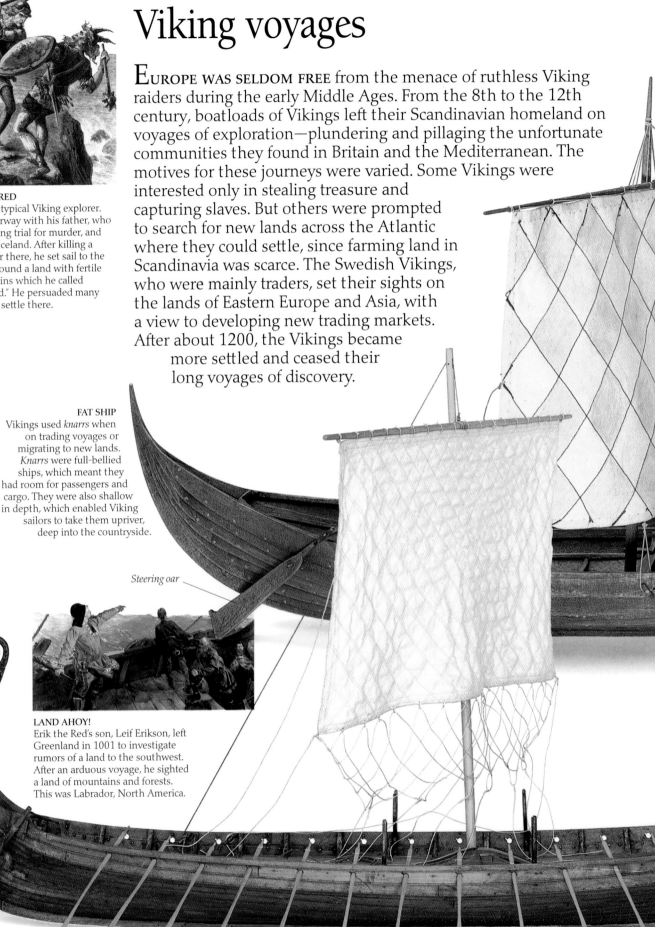

ERIK THE RED
Erik was a typical Viking explorer. He left Norway with his father, who was escaping trial for murder, and settled in Iceland. After killing a rival settler there, he set sail to the west and found a land with fertile coastal plains which he called "Greenland." He persuaded many Vikings to settle there.

FAT SHIP
Vikings used *knarrs* when on trading voyages or migrating to new lands. *Knarrs* were full-bellied ships, which meant they had room for passengers and cargo. They were also shallow in depth, which enabled Viking sailors to take them upriver, deep into the countryside.

Steering oar

LAND AHOY!
Erik the Red's son, Leif Erikson, left Greenland in 1001 to investigate rumors of a land to the southwest. After an arduous voyage, he sighted a land of mountains and forests. This was Labrador, North America.

Steering oar

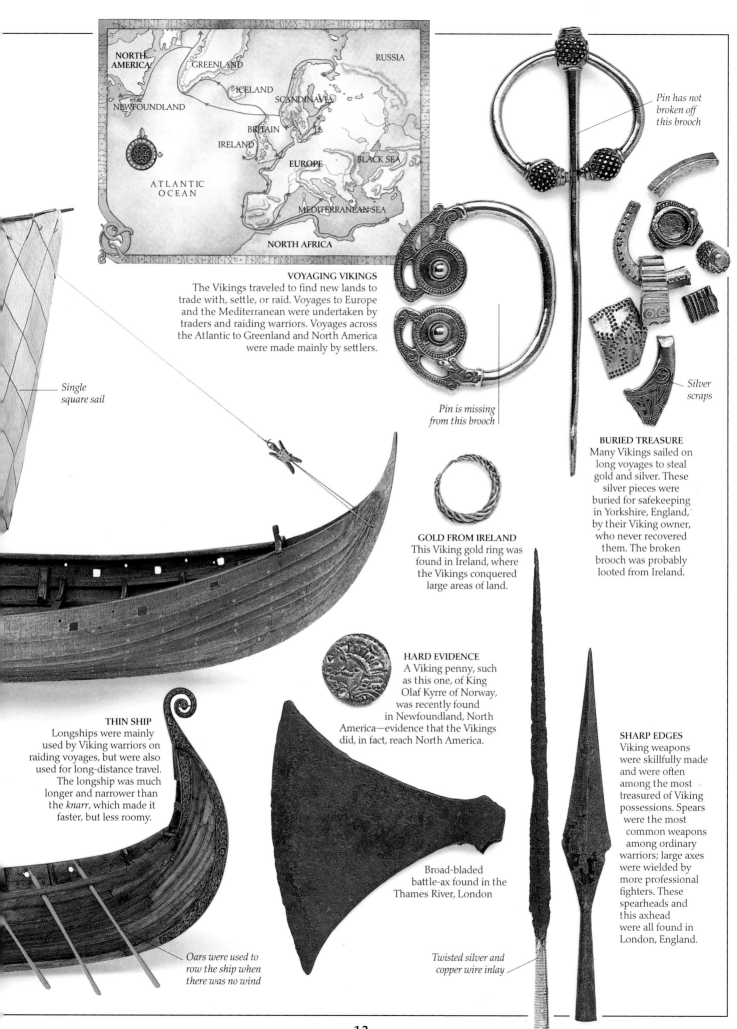

VOYAGING VIKINGS
The Vikings traveled to find new lands to trade with, settle, or raid. Voyages to Europe and the Mediterranean were undertaken by traders and raiding warriors. Voyages across the Atlantic to Greenland and North America were made mainly by settlers.

Pin has not broken off this brooch

Silver scraps

BURIED TREASURE
Many Vikings sailed on long voyages to steal gold and silver. These silver pieces were buried for safekeeping in Yorkshire, England, by their Viking owner, who never recovered them. The broken brooch was probably looted from Ireland.

Single square sail

Pin is missing from this brooch

GOLD FROM IRELAND
This Viking gold ring was found in Ireland, where the Vikings conquered large areas of land.

HARD EVIDENCE
A Viking penny, such as this one, of King Olaf Kyrre of Norway, was recently found in Newfoundland, North America—evidence that the Vikings did, in fact, reach North America.

THIN SHIP
Longships were mainly used by Viking warriors on raiding voyages, but were also used for long-distance travel. The longship was much longer and narrower than the *knarr*, which made it faster, but less roomy.

SHARP EDGES
Viking weapons were skillfully made and were often among the most treasured of Viking possessions. Spears were the most common weapons among ordinary warriors; large axes were wielded by more professional fighters. These spearheads and this axhead were all found in London, England.

Oars were used to row the ship when there was no wind

Broad-bladed battle-ax found in the Thames River, London

Twisted silver and copper wire inlay

Polynesian settlers

Large, double canoe used by migrating families

WHEN EUROPEANS FIRST REACHED the remote islands of the Pacific Ocean (pp. 62–63), they found them already inhabited by a people called the Polynesians. These were a seafaring people who, at about the same time as the Phoenicians were exploring the Mediterranean (pp. 6–7), were "island-hopping" thousands of miles eastward across the Pacific. They traveled in relatively small canoes that were nevertheless strong and stable, and were expert seamen and navigators who could deduce the direction of land from the shape and size of waves and from the behavior of sea creatures. Historians think the main reason for these long voyages of exploration was to find new islands to colonize. The Polynesian population was a large one, and as one island became too crowded, some families would set off in search of the next island.

BIRD AND WAVES
The Polynesians lavished great care on their canoes. This elaborately carved wooden prowboard features a bird and waves and would have been attached to the prow of a large canoe.

Waves

Cowrie shell

POLYNESIAN PADDLE
This finely carved canoe paddle comes from New Zealand. You can see paddles like this in use in the picture at the top of this page.

MODERN CANOE *left*
This modern racing canoe from Papua New Guinea (pp. 62–63) incorporates many features of traditional Polynesian design. Though made of fiberglass, the canoe is the same shape and has a similar outrigger attached for stability.

SHORT-HAUL CANOE *below*
This model shows a small canoe as used by the Polynesians for shorter voyages between neighboring islands and for fishing. The main hull is made from a log, which has been hollowed out, and the small outrigger adds stability by making the base of the canoe bigger.

Outrigger

LUCKY FISHING
The Polynesians believed that every occupation or place had its own god or spirit. This canoe god from the Cook Islands brought good luck to fishermen.

RELAXING BY THE SEA
European explorers found that the Polynesians enjoyed their warm and relaxing climate to the full!

Barbed point of spear was horribly effective

Polynesian spear

Human hair

Coconut fiber

SHELL NECKLACE
This necklace, made from shell, coconut fiber, and human hair, is also from the Cook Islands. Showy ornaments such as this were worn only by chiefs and their families.

Shell

WEAPONS OF WAR
Polynesians lived in a violent society. Warfare and feuding were common; sometimes quarrels continued from one generation to the next and claimed the lives of hundreds of people before they were forgotten. The weapons used by Polynesian warriors were simple, but brutally effective. Tribal armies fought with great discipline and courage, sometimes preferring annihilation (destruction) to the shame of surrender.

Polynesian war club

Shark's tooth

Hair

SWAYING SKIRT *above*
This Polynesian "grass" skirt is actually made from the inner bark of the hibiscus plant (pp. 50–51). Lightweight clothing like this was comfortable in the warm climate and allowed easy movement.

Fiji islander in dance costume

HAIRY COMB
Polynesians decorated their combs with braided human hair.

Polynesian dagger

The Silk Road

A camel train

NOT ALL EXPLORATION took place over rolling seas. One of the oldest and most important land routes, the Silk Road, was forged around 500 BCE and was used until sea routes to China were opened up in about 1650. Along this road, trade was conducted between China and Europe. Chinese merchants sent silk and spices westward to Europe over the fearsome mountains and deserts of Asia, while gold, silver, and horses were imported to China. However, no one traveled the entire length of the Silk Road until Marco Polo in the 13th century. The road was about 4,300 miles (7,000 km) long and very dangerous, and no one knew for certain what was at the other end. It passed through numerous kingdoms where each ruler demanded money or gifts from travelers. In addition, bandits would often pillage a traveling camel train. Because of these dangers, silk was passed from one merchant to another, with no trader traveling for more than a few hundred miles at a time! The Silk Road declined in importance after European ships began a regular trade with China around the southern tip of Africa.

PURCHASING POWER
Chinese silk and porcelain were very popular in Europe. These Spanish silver coins were sent to China in exchange for Chinese goods. On many of them you can see marks where Chinese merchants cut into them to check that they were solid silver!

Check marks

Turkish silver mount on rim

Dragon handles

SUMPTUOUS SILK
The most important product traded along the Silk Road was, of course, silk—like this cloth here. For centuries, the Chinese kept from other nations the secret of how silk was made.

14th-century Yuan dynasty jar

16th-century Chinese plate made for the Portuguese market

Portuguese galleon motif

ORIENTAL PORCELAIN
Porcelain is a very hard, translucent (allows light to pass through) pottery invented by the Chinese. It was too fragile to transport in bulk along the Silk Road, but small pieces were traded, since it was in high demand. It was not until the sea routes opened up in the 17th century that trade in porcelain began in earnest.

14th- to 15th-century Ming dynasty bowl found in Kenya

ANY OLD JUNK?
Large Chinese ships called *junks* sailed to the Indonesian islands (pp. 62–63) in order to trade for spices. *Junks* had flat bottoms to enable them to carry a lot of cargo. Some of these ships may have reached the northern Australian coast.

Wooden strips to stiffen sails

The Chinese explorer Cheng Ho probably sailed in *junks* like this one during his voyages to India and East Africa (1404–33)

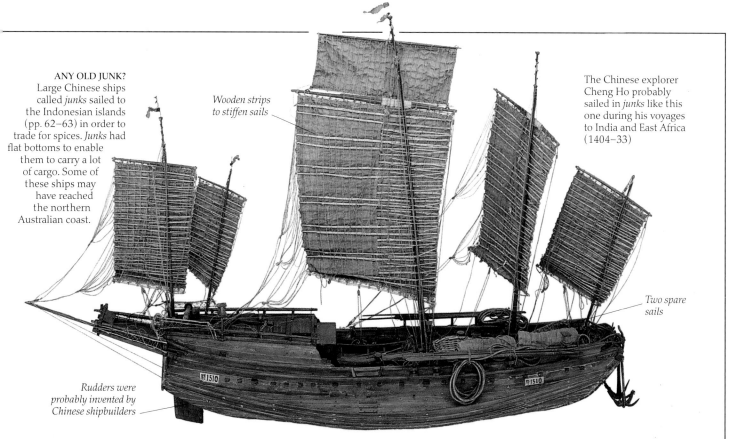

Two spare sails

Rudders were probably invented by Chinese shipbuilders

THE RUSSIAN OFFICER
Nicolay Przhevalsky was a Russian army officer who grew bored with soldiering and became an explorer instead. In 1867, he led a military expedition to explore vast areas of Central Asia. He later led four expeditions into unknown regions of Central Asia, where he discovered kingdoms and countries previously unknown to Europeans.

This detail from a 17th-century Dutch map shows merchants in the East

TREACHEROUS ROUTE
This map shows the Silk Road and route of Marco Polo (see below). He used the Silk Road to cross Asia, which took him four years. He braved bandits, disease, and desert before returning by sea to Persia and then to Venice. He wrote an account of his travels, which many Europeans thought was too fabulous to be true!

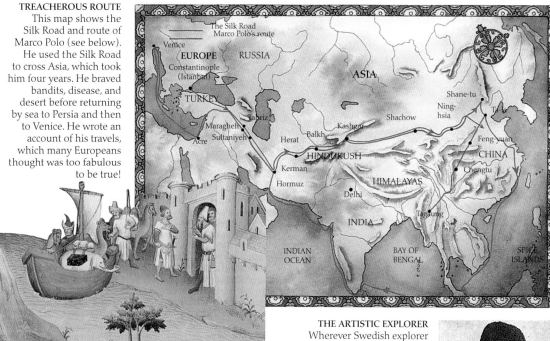

The Silk Road
Marco Polo's route

Venice
EUROPE RUSSIA
Constantinople (Istanbul)
TURKEY
ASIA
Tabriz
Maragheh
Sultaniyeh
Acre
Herat
Balkh
Kashgar
Shachow
Shane-tu
Ning-hsia
Ta-lu
HINDUKUSH
Kerman
Feng-yuan
CHINA
Hormuz
Chengtu
HIMALAYAS
Delhi
Tagaung
INDIA
INDIAN OCEAN
BAY OF BENGAL
SPICE ISLANDS

MARCO POLO
In 1271, a Venetian merchant named Marco Polo traveled to China along the Silk Road with his father and uncle, who had already visited the Chinese emperor Kublai Khan. He spent several years in China working as a government official before returning to Venice. This picture shows the Polos arriving at the Muslim city of Hormuz in the Persian Gulf.

THE ARTISTIC EXPLORER
Wherever Swedish explorer Sven Hedin traveled, he sketched and painted what he saw. Between 1890 and 1934, Hedin made several journeys into Central Asia, exploring and mapping new regions. He was twice held prisoner by bandits, and once nearly died of thirst.

OOST INDIEN

WASSENDE-GRAADE PASKAART,

Arab adventurers

ARAB WARRIORS TRAVELED vast distances to conquer an empire that stretched from northern Spain across North Africa to northwest India in the sixth and seventh centuries. These holy wars were launched to spread the Islamic faith, and many Muslim communities were established. Arab merchants also pushed out in all directions to find new trading areas. Some Arab traders traveled across the Sahara on camel and penetrated central Asia on horseback. By the 13th century, Arabs were using *dhows* to sail across the Indian Ocean to purchase silks, spices, and jewels from India, Indonesia, and China. Other ships sailed down the East African coast to collect slaves (pp. 46–47), ivory, and gold.

An Arab street trader

SLAVE TRADE
Much of the Arab wealth came from slave trading. Some prisoners were captured in Europe and Asia, but most came from Africa. They were captured in battles or bought from local tribesmen and then taken back to North Africa, where they were sold to noblemen or craftsmen.

MARCHING CHAINS
The Arab slave trade continued up until the late 19th century, when European powers took over most of Africa (pp. 46–47). The slaves captured inland were locked into chains for the long marches to the coast.

ARABIC QUADRANT
One of the earliest navigational instruments invented by Arabs, the quadrant was a quarter circle with a plumbline attached.

Approximate latitude was calculated by lining up one straight side on a heavenly body and reading off the position of the plumbline

Quadrant was made of wood or brass

Written instructions

EVER-LASTING *DHOWS*
Dhows have been used for centuries by Muslim traders in the Persian Gulf and Indian Ocean and are still in use today. They have triangular lateen sails rigged on one or two masts and are able to sail very close to the wind. They can also be handled by a small crew. Most of the early Arab voyages of exploration or trade were made in *dhows*.

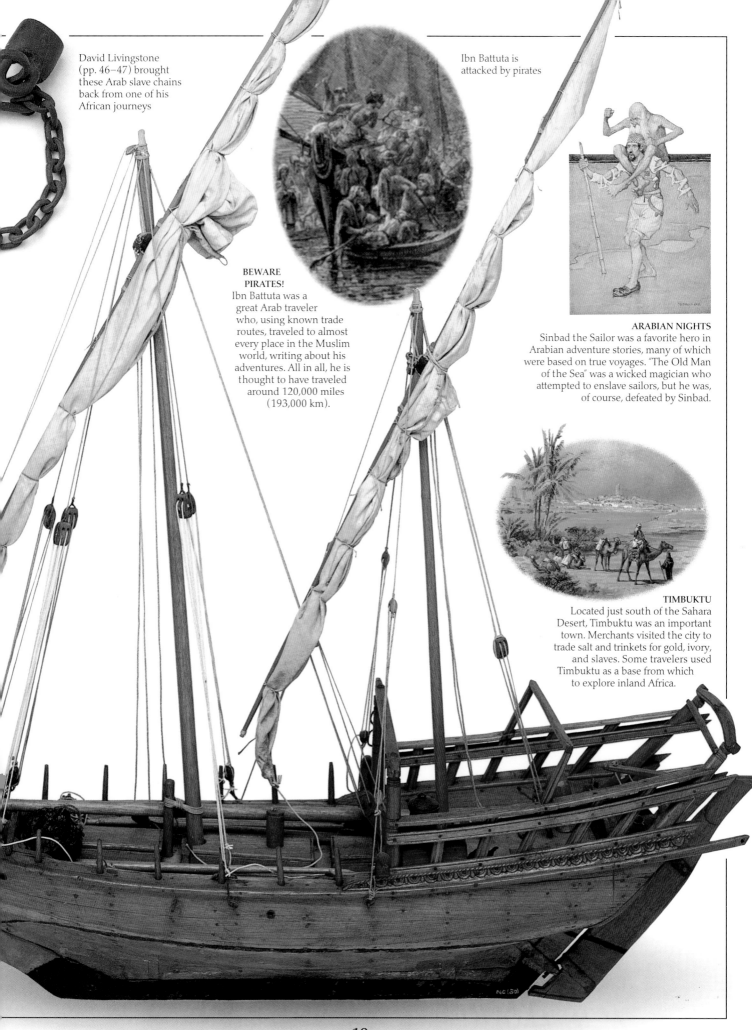

David Livingstone
(pp. 46–47) brought
these Arab slave chains
back from one of his
African journeys

Ibn Battuta is
attacked by pirates

**BEWARE
PIRATES!**
Ibn Battuta was a
great Arab traveler
who, using known trade
routes, traveled to almost
every place in the Muslim
world, writing about his
adventures. All in all, he is
thought to have traveled
around 120,000 miles
(193,000 km).

ARABIAN NIGHTS
Sinbad the Sailor was a favorite hero in
Arabian adventure stories, many of which
were based on true voyages. "The Old Man
of the Sea" was a wicked magician who
attempted to enslave sailors, but he was,
of course, defeated by Sinbad.

TIMBUKTU
Located just south of the Sahara
Desert, Timbuktu was an important
town. Merchants visited the city to
trade salt and trinkets for gold, ivory,
and slaves. Some travelers used
Timbuktu as a base from which
to explore inland Africa.

The Age of Exploration

It was in early 15th-century Portugal that the first great voyages of "the Age of Exploration" began. In 1415, Prince Henry of Portugal—known as "Henry the Navigator"—was given command of the port of Ceuta (northern Morocco) and its ships. He used these ships to explore the west coast of Africa and paid for numerous expeditions that eventually reached Sierra Leone on Africa's northwest coast. Later kings of Portugal financed expeditions that rounded the Cape of Good Hope on the southern tip of Africa, and this led to the setting up of trading routes to India, China, and the Indonesian and Philippine islands—"the Spice Islands." These links made Portugal immensely rich and powerful through its control of trade in this area.

PRINCE HENRY
Henry the Navigator only sailed on two voyages himself. However, he financed many voyages of exploration up to 1460 and founded a Portuguese school of navigation.

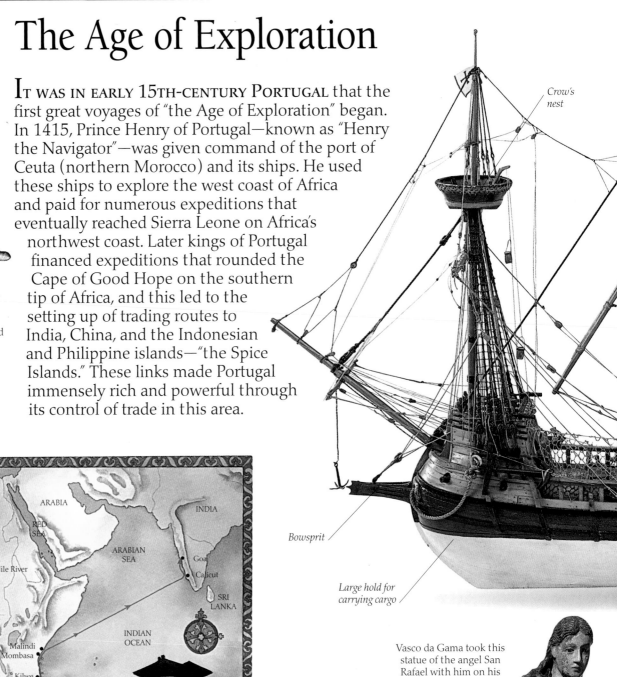

Crow's nest

Bowsprit

Large hold for carrying cargo

Vasco da Gama's route to India

PASSAGE TO INDIA
Vasco da Gama's route took him via the Cape of Good Hope. He then sailed north along the east coast of Africa until he reached Malindi. There he took on board an Arab navigator who showed da Gama how to use the monsoon winds to cross the Indian Ocean—and reach India.

Vasco da Gama took this statue of the angel San Rafael with him on his trip to India in 1498

VASCO DA GAMA
Famous as the first European to sail to India, Vasco da Gama made his historic voyage around the Cape of Good Hope to India in 1497 and arrived in India in 1498. Two years later, a trading station established in India by the Portuguese was destroyed by local Muslims. Da Gama led a fleet of warships to exact revenge, and in 1502 his fleet destroyed the town of Calicut. In 1524, da Gama was appointed Portuguese viceroy in India, but died almost as soon as he arrived to take up his post.

AFRICAN IVORY
Once sea routes from Portugal to Africa had been opened up, Portuguese traders flocked to West Africa to collect ivory. This ivory statue was made by a West African craftsman in the 17th century and shows a Portuguese sailor in a crow's nest.

PORTUGUESE ENTERPRISE
In 1469, the Portuguese king granted Fernao Gomes trading rights with West Africa—on the condition that he explore 350 miles (555 km) of coast each year. This map shows the coastline he had discovered by 1475.

TIN COIN
By the end of the 16th century, Portugal's considerable trading interests had led to the formation of a large Portuguese empire in the East. This Portuguese tin coin was minted in Malaya (now Malaysia) in 1511.

THE FAVORITE SHIP
Most early Portuguese explorers made their voyages in small wooden sailing ships called "caravels." These sturdy ships were able to withstand storms and had large holds for carrying cargo. Their lateen (triangular) sails enabled them to take advantage of a wind blowing from the side of the ship.

AZIMUTH COMPASS
This beautifully decorated Portuguese marine compass was made in 1780, but it incorporates the design of much earlier compasses.

MARK OF THE CROSS
In 1487, Bartolomeu Diaz became the first European to make a confirmed passage around the Cape of Good Hope, Africa. Before leaving, he erected a cross on the Cape to mark his discovery.

The New World

EVEN THE MOST EDUCATED Europeans knew little about the world outside Europe in 1480. South of the Sahara Desert in North Africa stretched vast, impenetrable jungles. Asia was rarely visited, and the stories that travelers brought back were so amazing that few people believed them (pp. 16–17). To the west lay the vast Atlantic Ocean, but no one knew how wide the Atlantic was or what lay on the other side. Then, in 1480, the Italian navigator Christopher Columbus announced that he had calculated that the East Indies lay just 2,795 miles (4,500km) to the west. Few believed him, and indeed it was later proved that he was wrong. Nevertheless, the Spanish king and queen paid for his expedition, and Columbus discovered America where he thought the East Indies should be. This voyage was one of the most important that took place during the Age of Exploration (pp. 20–21).

THE FIRST SEA ATLAS
In 1582, the Dutchman Lucas Wagenaer published a book containing detailed information about the coasts of western Europe. The frontispiece (above) was beautifully decorated with ships and nautical instruments.

HANGING BEDS
When Columbus and his men reached the West Indies, they found the natives sleeping in hanging beds called "hamacas." The sailors copied this idea to make dry, rat-free beds above the dirty and wet decks. We now call these beds "hammocks."

SIR WALTER RALEIGH
During the late 16th century, Sir Walter Raleigh tried unsuccessfully to establish English colonies in the "New World" that Columbus had found. However, he is usually remembered more for the potatoes and tobacco plants that his captains brought back to England!

SWEET FRUITS
The New World discovered by Columbus was inhabited by peoples who grew crops very different from those in Europe. These included pineapples and sweet potatoes, which were taken back to Europe.

REWARDS OF SUCCESS
When Christopher Columbus returned from his first voyage, he brought back strange people and objects from the New World to present to King Ferdinand and Queen Isabella. They were so impressed that they made Columbus an admiral and a nobleman.

Royal flag
of Spain

AMERIGO'S LAND
"America" gets its name from
"Amerigo's land," which was used
on a map made in 1507 by Martin
Waldseemuller. The mapmaker named
the land after Italian navigator
Amerigo Vespucci, having read
accounts of Vespucci's
voyages to the "New
World" and not realizing
that Columbus had
arrived there first.

**SETTING
A COURSE**
Columbus
took an astrolabe
similar to this on his voyage of
discovery but preferred to work
out his position at sea by "dead
reckoning"—keeping records of his
ship's speed and direction.

THE SANTA MARIA
The flagship of
Columbus's voyage was
the *Santa Maria*, a caravel from
northern Spain. Like the other two
ships of the expedition, the *Nina* and
the *Pinta*, it was short and stocky with
three masts. Columbus traveled on the
Santa Maria, but when it was wrecked
off the West Indies, he transferred to
the *Nina* for the voyage home.

NEW WORLD MAP
Columbus made four voyages to the New World. Most of
his time was spent exploring the West Indies, but on his third
voyage he reached the mainland near Panama, Central America.

NEW WORLD GOLD
In return for financing the
expedition, Columbus promised to
bring back gold for King Ferdinand
and Queen Isabella of Spain.
However, little gold was discovered
until Cortés reached the Aztec
Empire in 1519 (pp. 30–31).

PORTUGAL
Lisbon SPAIN
Palos

NORTH
AMERICA

GULF OF
MEXICO
WEST INDIES
Cuba
First voyage (1492–93)
SAHARA
DESERT

Jamaica   Haiti
ATLANTIC OCEAN
AFRICA

Third voyage (1498)

PACIFIC
OCEAN
Panama SOUTH AMERICA

Around the world

ALTHOUGH FERDINAND MAGELLAN is credited with having made the first voyage around the world, he did not actually complete the journey himself. Of the five ships that made up his fleet, only one, the *Vittoria*, returned after a grueling three-year journey, and Magellan was not on board. Ferdinand Magellan was a Portuguese gentleman who, like Christopher Columbus before him (pp. 22–23), thought he could navigate a westward route to the Spice Islands of the East. By 1500, Portugal had established a sea route to the Spice Islands around the Cape of Good Hope (pp. 62–63). Spain was eager to join in the highly profitable trade Portugal enjoyed with these islands, and in 1519, the king commissioned Magellan to forge his westward route. Magellan's journey took him through the dangerous, stormy passage at the tip of South America, now called the Strait of Magellan. On emerging into the calm ocean on the other side, Magellan referred to it as "the sea of peace," or Pacific Ocean. He was the first European to sail from the Atlantic Ocean to the Pacific Ocean.

MONSTER AHOY!
Sailors of Magellan's time were terrified of huge, serpentine beasts they believed capable of eating men and sinking ships.

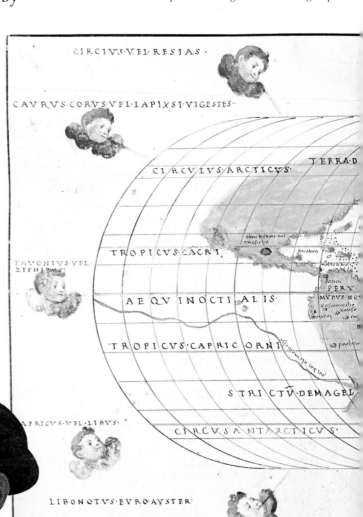

CIRCLING THE EARTH
Battista Agnese's map was drawn after the return of the *Vittoria*. Magellan's route through the Strait of Magellan is shown, but the extent of the land to the south remains unclear. The approximate size of the Pacific Ocean is indicated, though Australia and most of the Pacific islands are missing.

Antonio Pigafetta's 16th-century manuscript showing Magellan's journey

FERDINAND MAGELLAN
Ferdinand Magellan was a Portuguese adventurer of noble parentage. In 1518, he persuaded Charles I of Spain that he could reach the Spice Islands in the East by sailing around Cape Horn, and so across the Pacific Ocean. He succeeded in reaching the islands, but became involved in a local war on one of them and was killed in battle.

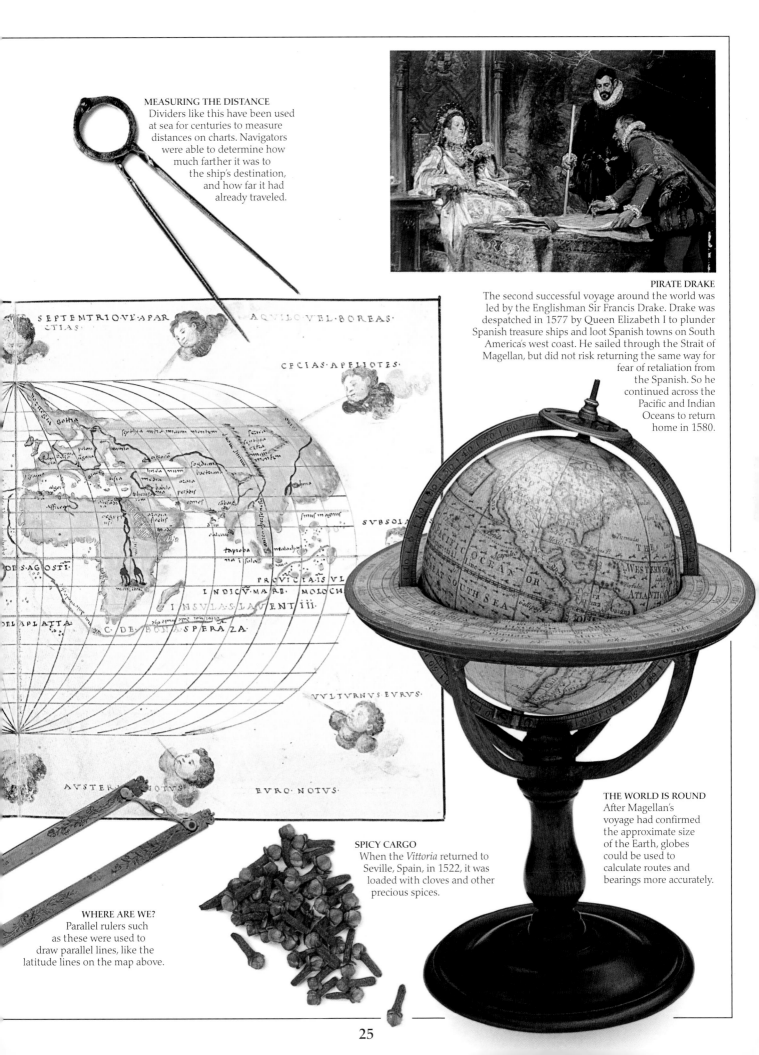

MEASURING THE DISTANCE
Dividers like this have been used at sea for centuries to measure distances on charts. Navigators were able to determine how much farther it was to the ship's destination, and how far it had already traveled.

PIRATE DRAKE
The second successful voyage around the world was led by the Englishman Sir Francis Drake. Drake was despatched in 1577 by Queen Elizabeth I to plunder Spanish treasure ships and loot Spanish towns on South America's west coast. He sailed through the Strait of Magellan, but did not risk returning the same way for fear of retaliation from the Spanish. So he continued across the Pacific and Indian Oceans to return home in 1580.

THE WORLD IS ROUND
After Magellan's voyage had confirmed the approximate size of the Earth, globes could be used to calculate routes and bearings more accurately.

SPICY CARGO
When the *Vittoria* returned to Seville, Spain, in 1522, it was loaded with cloves and other precious spices.

WHERE ARE WE?
Parallel rulers such as these were used to draw parallel lines, like the latitude lines on the map above.

25

Life at sea

BEFORE THE INTRODUCTION of modern luxuries, life on board ship was hard for the ordinary sailor. Long voyages often involved being at sea for months—even years. Fresh food was unobtainable, and even drinking water could be scarce. Terrible diseases—particularly scurvy (vitamin deficiency)—were common, resulting in many deaths at sea. The sailor's numerous duties included climbing the high masts and rigging to work the sails (often in the most hazardous weather conditions), taking turns on watch, and swabbing down filthy decks at regular intervals.

Seamen spent what time they did have to themselves on hobbies or games or on playing pranks on fellow crew members. Life on board ship changed little between 1500 and 1850. After this, the introduction of steam power and more sophisticated navigational aids made the sailor's life much more bearable.

Sailors in rigging

PASSING THE TIME
Seamen on whaling ships often passed their spare time engraving designs on whales' teeth. The engraving was sometimes rubbed with black ink or soot to produce a clear image. This art is known as "scrimshaw."

SAILOR'S SEA CHEST
Sailors stored all their belongings in a sea chest, which took up little room on board. These chests had to be strong, since they had a variety of uses; they were sometimes used as seats, tables, and even beds. This chest has the name and date of its owner painted on it and is full of the kind of objects it might have originally held.

GOLD HOOPS
Sailors sometimes wore earrings. This gold pair belonged to a 19th-century American sailor named Richard Ward.

18th-century log slate

SEA BED
The hammock was adapted from a hanging bed Columbus discovered (pp. 22–23). Because the hammock swings from side to side, it did not tip out its occupant in heavy seas.

Sailor's hat

Pencil for slate

Twist of tobacco

Penknife

Sailmaker's bag

Fid for splicing ropes

Seam rubber for flattening seams

Palm to protect hand

Needles and case

TOOLS OF THE TRADE
Few skills were more essential than that of the sailmaker. This bag contains the tools necessary for mending sails, repairing ropes, and sewing canvas.

BOSUN'S WHISTLE
The bosun's whistle was used to pass on orders at sea. Its high-pitched tone could be heard over the noise of wind and waves better than the human voice. Loudspeakers have now replaced the whistle, but it is still used on ceremonial occasions.

Silver 18th-century whistle

Logbook

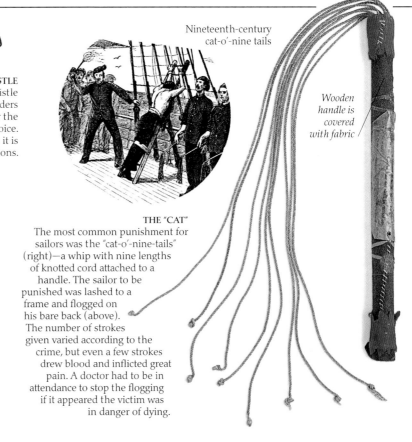

Nineteenth-century cat-o'-nine tails

Wooden handle is covered with fabric

THE "CAT"
The most common punishment for sailors was the "cat-o'-nine-tails" (right)—a whip with nine lengths of knotted cord attached to a handle. The sailor to be punished was lashed to a frame and flogged on his bare back (above). The number of strokes given varied according to the crime, but even a few strokes drew blood and inflicted great pain. A doctor had to be in attendance to stop the flogging if it appeared the victim was in danger of dying.

Pewter cup and plate

Hardtack

Bone-handled steel fork

Food fit for a sailor

Before the days of canning and refrigeration, storing food on board ship was a great problem. Fresh fruit and vegetables rotted quickly, and meat was salted and stored in barrels. Hardtack was a form of cracker that kept for years. These cracker often became infested with beetles or maggots, which had to be removed before the crackers could be eaten!

WATERPROOF PANTS
Sailors often made clothes from spare materials found on board ship. These pants are made of canvas left over from sail repairs and have been treated with oil to make them waterproof.

BOWING TO NEPTUNE
Sailors crossing the equator for the first time had to undergo "the Neptune Ceremony." This varied, but usually involved the sailor having to bow to a shipmate dressed as the sea god Neptune. The unfortunate man was then forced to drink an unpleasant liquid before being dunked in a tub of seawater.

Tricks of the trade

Star
Scale
Crosspiece
Horizon
Cross-staff
in use

MODERN NAVIGATORS USE RADAR, radio, and satellites continuously to update the position of their ships as they move. Before these inventions, navigation involved careful manual calculation. Navigators used instruments designed for observing the heavens and related what they saw to a sea chart. They then took a reasonably short but safe course between two defined points, taking into account wind direction, currents, and rocks. Until nautical almanacs and marine chronometers were introduced in the 1760s, it was virtually impossible to find a ship's longitude. Navigators had to rely on estimates of their course and speed to guess their longtitude (that is, "dead reckoning"), and observations of the Sun or the North Star to figure out their latitude (a useful corrective to dead reckoning).

Spare
crosspiece

Scale

Cross-staff

LODESTONE
Before the invention of the compass, lodestone (naturally magnetic iron oxide) was used to determine direction. When suspended, lodestone always points north. About 2,000 years ago, the Chinese discovered that if they stroked a soft iron rod with lodestone, it too would point north.

Shadow vane

This backsight was positioned at the estimated latitude. The reading on the shadow vane was added to this to give the true latitude

Horizon slit

BACKSTAFF
The backstaff gave a ship's latitude by sighting on the Sun, which was too bright to gaze at long enough to use the cross-staff. The navigator stood with his back to the Sun, then lined up the backsight and the horizon slit. The shadow vane on the smaller arc was moved until its shadow fell on the horizon slit. The combined angles of the backsight and shadow vane gave the angle of the Sun and hence the latitude of the ship.

TELESCOPE
The telescope was invented simultaneously in Italy, Holland, and England in the early 17th century, and explorers quickly made use of it. By using the telescope, a traveler could identify landmarks or headlands from a great distance and so recognize his precise position. The marine telescope shown above was made in 1661.

JACOB CVNIGHAM
1 6 6 1

CROSS-STAFF
The cross-staff was used from the late 15th century onward to determine a ship's latitude. Navigators knew that the observed angle between the horizon and the North Star changed, depending on the latitude of the ship. By placing one end of the cross-staff against the eye, the navigator could slide the crosspiece along a scale until one end lined up with the horizon, and the other with the star. The ship's latitude could then be calculated.

Crosspiece

Astrolabe in use

Mirror

Mirror

SEXTANT
The sextant was invented in the mid-18th century by the British Navy to replace the backstaff and cross-staff. Using an arrangement of mirrors, the sextant can measure latitude to an accuracy of 0.01 of a degree. The navigator moves the index bar until the mirrors appear to line up the Sun with the horizon. By reading the angle of the index bar, the angle of the Sun (and therefore the ship's latitude) can be calculated.

MOORISH ASTROLABE
The astrolabe was developed by Arab astronomers as a two-dimensional model of the heavens. On one side (shown in the little picture) a pointer could be aligned so that a sunbeam or star was visible through two tiny holes on the alidade, or central rod, while the pointer marked its angular height on an engraved scale.

Index bar

Sextant in use

Sextant that Captain Cook used on his third voyage to the Pacific (pp. 34–35)

COMPASS *below*
From the 12th century, magnetic compasses were used by seafaring explorers to define their courses and to determine in which direction to steer. Early compasses were magnetized needles that pointed north when suspended on string. Later, the needle was balanced on a central pivot and a card showing compass directions was mounted on top (as shown in the example below).

SHIP'S LOGBOOK
All ship's captains keep a logbook, which they write up each day. In it they record how far the ship has traveled and in which direction. The captain will also mention any events, such as other ships sighted, landmarks passed, or sickness among the crew.

This log dated 1770 was beautifully kept with pictures of passing ships and headlands

Gold and the gospel

W HEN COLUMBUS SET SAIL across the Atlantic (pp. 22–23) he hoped to discover a new trade route to China and the Spice Islands. Instead he found the West Indies—islands inhabited by tribes with a relatively simple culture. These "Indians" had a few gold trinkets, but not much else of value. In 1519, in the hope of establishing a trading colony on the mainland, Spain sent Hernando Cortés to Veracruz, Mexico. Cortés was staggered to be met by richly dressed "ambassadors" who gave him valuable gifts of gold. However, not content with these, Cortés resolved to travel inland in search of even greater riches. These he found when he reached the mighty Aztec Empire, which, in little more than two years, he and his troops totally destroyed. A similar fate awaited the equally wealthy Inca Empire of Peru, South America, which another Spaniard—Francisco Pizarro—conquered in 1532. Consumed with the greed for gold, many Spaniards followed. Large areas were explored by these "conquistadors" and several Spanish colonies were established.

Aztec gold figure

Aztec warriors earned the right to wear animal costumes by taking many prisoners

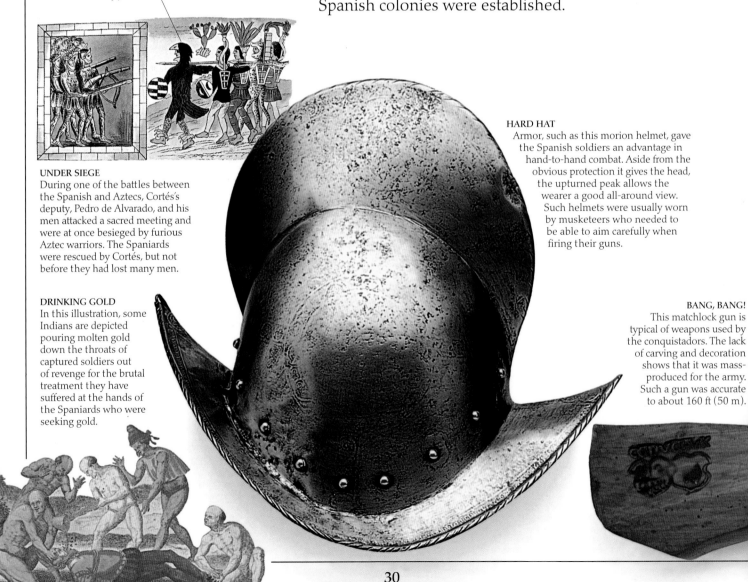

UNDER SIEGE
During one of the battles between the Spanish and Aztecs, Cortés's deputy, Pedro de Alvarado, and his men attacked a sacred meeting and were at once besieged by furious Aztec warriors. The Spaniards were rescued by Cortés, but not before they had lost many men.

DRINKING GOLD
In this illustration, some Indians are depicted pouring molten gold down the throats of captured soldiers out of revenge for the brutal treatment they have suffered at the hands of the Spaniards who were seeking gold.

HARD HAT
Armor, such as this morion helmet, gave the Spanish soldiers an advantage in hand-to-hand combat. Aside from the obvious protection it gives the head, the upturned peak allows the wearer a good all-around view. Such helmets were usually worn by musketeers who needed to be able to aim carefully when firing their guns.

BANG, BANG!
This matchlock gun is typical of weapons used by the conquistadors. The lack of carving and decoration shows that it was mass-produced for the army. Such a gun was accurate to about 160 ft (50 m).

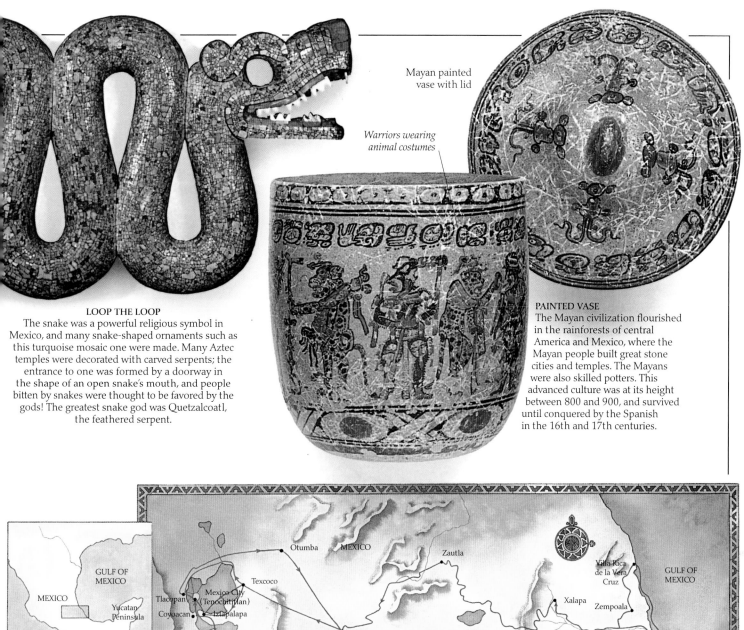

LOOP THE LOOP

The snake was a powerful religious symbol in Mexico, and many snake-shaped ornaments such as this turquoise mosaic one were made. Many Aztec temples were decorated with carved serpents; the entrance to one was formed by a doorway in the shape of an open snake's mouth, and people bitten by snakes were thought to be favored by the gods! The greatest snake god was Quetzalcoatl, the feathered serpent.

Mayan painted vase with lid

Warriors wearing animal costumes

PAINTED VASE

The Mayan civilization flourished in the rainforests of central America and Mexico, where the Mayan people built great stone cities and temples. The Mayans were also skilled potters. This advanced culture was at its height between 800 and 900, and survived until conquered by the Spanish in the 16th and 17th centuries.

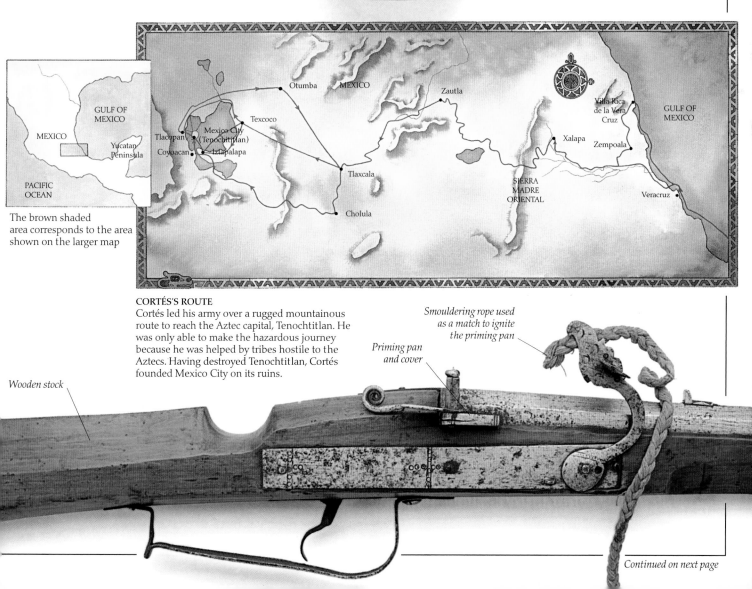

The brown shaded area corresponds to the area shown on the larger map

CORTÉS'S ROUTE

Cortés led his army over a rugged mountainous route to reach the Aztec capital, Tenochtitlan. He was only able to make the hazardous journey because he was helped by tribes hostile to the Aztecs. Having destroyed Tenochtitlan, Cortés founded Mexico City on its ruins.

Wooden stock

Priming pan and cover

Smouldering rope used as a match to ignite the priming pan

Continued on next page

GOLD DOUBLOONS
Mexico and Peru were enormously rich in gold and silver. Much of the gold mined by the Spanish in South America was made into gold coins that were shipped back to Spain.

18th-century gold doubloons

Lion and castle, symbols of the Spanish crown

Pillars of Hercules, symbol of the Spanish Empire

A Spanish conquistador— maybe Pizarro himself—is depicted on the cup

WOODEN CUP
This wooden cup was made by an Incan craftsman in the mid-16th century. It was sent back to Spain after Pizarro's murder in 1541 by fellow Spanish soldiers in a personal feud. The Inca Empire was governed by Pizarro for eight years, during which time he imposed European administration and industry on the proud Incan Indians.

DEATH OF A KING
At his first meeting with the great Incan king, Atahualpa, Pizarro made a surprise attack and captured the king. Although Atahualpa paid a vast ransom, Pizarro could not risk freeing him and had him executed.

Quinoa shoot

Quinoa grain

"GRAIN OF THE GODS"
The food the Incas ate was rather plain and simple. Meals often consisted of roasted or boiled corn, potatoes, and this grain called "quinoa," also called "grain of the gods."

TELL OR ELSE!
In 1539, Hernando de Soto landed in Florida and marched north in the never-ending Spanish search for gold. De Soto found no treasure, but was convinced that the local Indians were hiding their gold from him. He subjected them to incredibly cruel tortures in the hope that they would reveal where they had hidden the gold.

CRUEL RELIGION
The Aztec religion seems very cruel to us; several Aztec gods demanded blood sacrifices. Humans sacrificed to the war god Huitzilopochtli had their still-beating hearts cut out with a knife.

THE LAST CONQUISTADOR
In 1540, rumors of a rich city far to the north led to a large expedition headed by Francisco Coronado. He marched through much of what is now the United States, reaching the Kansas River and discovering the Grand Canyon. However, Coronado found neither gold nor city.

Catholics use a string of beads called a rosary for counting prayers

The Gospel

The Catholic religion was of vital importance to the Spanish conquistadors. All Spanish expeditions were accompanied by a priest, who was expected both to conduct religious services and to convert to Christianity any "heathens" they encountered. Both priests and soldiers were disgusted by the religions they came across in the New World; human sacrifice was common, as was the worship of idols. The Spanish set about systematically destroying temples and executing local priests, which led to the total disruption of the Aztec and Incan societies. The policy was so widespread and complete that today the principal religion in Central and South America is Catholicism.

The Great South Sea

ALMOST ALL THE MYSTERIES surrounding the southern and central Pacific, "the Great South Sea," were solved during the late 18th century. Until then, Australia's east coast was unknown, and the two islands of New Zealand were thought to be one. However, in 1768, an excellent navigator and cartographer (map drawer) named James Cook set sail from Plymouth, England (pp. 36–37). The task set for him by the Admiralty was to explore and chart the region. During this voyage, he charted the New Zealand coasts and Australia's east coast. His next voyage, in 1772, took him to Antarctica and many Pacific islands, and his third, in 1776, led to the discovery of the Hawaiian islands and exploration of the Alaskan coast.

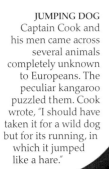

CAPTAIN JAMES COOK
This portrait of James Cook was painted after his return from his second voyage. His wife thought it was a good likeness, but considered his expression "a little too severe."

Dividers

Penholder

Dividers

Parallel ruler

Sector

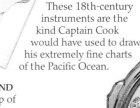

ABEL TASMAN
During the 17th century, the Dutchman Abel Tasman sailed around the southern coast of Australia, without seeing it, and discovered New Zealand and Fiji.

DRAWING TOOLS
These 18th-century instruments are the kind Captain Cook would have used to draw his extremely fine charts of the Pacific Ocean.

UNKNOWN LAND
This Dutch map of around 1590 shows a land labeled "Terra Australis Nondum Cognita," which means "Unknown Southern Land." Scientists argued over whether this southern land was one large land mass.

SEA TIME
An accurate timepiece was essential for determining a ship's longitude. This chronometer was used by Cook on his second voyage.

JUMPING DOG
Captain Cook and his men came across several animals completely unknown to Europeans. The peculiar kangaroo puzzled them. Cook wrote, "I should have taken it for a wild dog but for its running, in which it jumped like a hare."

DEATH OF COOK
Cook was always careful to maintain good relations with the native peoples he met. At first, the Hawaiians thought he was a god, but when one of Cook's men died, they realized he and his followers were mere mortals. The Hawaiians later stole a boat from Cook's ship, and when Cook went ashore to recover it, a scuffle broke out during which he was killed.

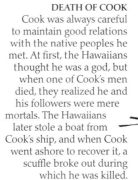

PORTABLE STOVE
Most meals on board ship were cooked in the galley, but the wealthy naturalist Sir Joseph Banks (pp. 50–51), who sailed on Cook's first voyage, prepared his own meals with this miniature stove.

SOLID SOUP
Cook was the first sea captain to take measures against scurvy. This soup tablet is made from marrow stock. When mixed with hot water, it made a nourishing soup that was thought to help prevent scurvy.

POLYNESIAN VILLAGE
This picture shows Nagaloa, a village in Fiji, as it appeared to early travelers.

FEATHER GORGET
The Polynesian kings and chiefs Cook met dressed in elaborate clothes made from the feathers of local birds. Cook brought back this magnificent "gorget," or chest ornament, worn by Tahitian kings.

BREADFRUIT
The large white fruits of the breadfruit tree that grows wild in Polynesia ripen easily and are a good source of food.

CARVED CRUSHER
Polynesian craftsmen were expert woodcarvers and produced many beautiful objects, such as this breadfruit pounder.

NO FLIES ON ME!
Polynesian society revolved around kings, queens, and nobles. Only important men and women were allowed to carry fly whisks like this. Strong religious rules called "taboos" forbade ordinary people to use such items.

The Endeavour

THE SHIP COOK CHOSE for his first voyage in 1768 (pp. 34–35) was the *Endeavour*, a rounded, tub-shaped coal-carrier. These coal-carriers were specially built to carry about 600 tons of coal from northern England to London. They had deep, broad waists, no figureheads, and narrow sterns. Cook had sailed in coal-carriers as a young man and so had experience of handling these strongly built ships. He knew that if he needed to he could beach the *Endeavour* without damaging it.

The Crew

As a naval vessel on scientific duty, the *Endeavour* had a mixed crew. In addition to Cook, there were several other officers to help navigate the ship and to make decisions. The sailors worked the ship and its rigging. Some sailors were skilled carpenters, sailmakers, musicians, or other craftsmen. The marines were armed soldiers who enforced discipline on the ship and protected the ship from pirates or hostile natives. Scientists and artists also traveled on the *Endeavour*. They did not help with the running of the ship, but spent their time making observations, conducting experiments, and sketching new sights.

Mizzenmast

Mainmast

Spanker

James Cook and Joseph Banks in cabin

British naval flag

1.

2.

3.

4.

5.

6.

7.

8.

9.

10.

11.

12.

13.

Coal

Planks of wood

Foremast

SHIP SPECIFICS
As a coal-carrier, the *Endeavour* was ship-rigged and capable of carrying a heavy cargo and many men. Ship-rigging meant that a ship had at least three square-rigged masts. The square sails were always turned to take the wind on one side only. The mizzen mast also carried a fore and aft sail that could take the wind on either side. This rig enabled the *Endeavour* to sail well in most types of weather and to survive the fiercest storms. The cargo hold could carry 600 tons and was specially converted for the voyage to contain supplies and scientific equipment. As the voyage continued, supplies were used up and replaced with plant and animal samples.

Bowsprit

SOME OF COOK'S CREW
1. Matthew Cox and Archibald Wolfe, seamen; 2. John Thompson, cook; 3. Herman Sporing, naturalist; 4. Sydney Parkinson, artist; 5. Alexander Buchan, artist; 6. Thomas Simmonds, seaman; 7. John Reynolds, servant; 8. William Monkhouse, surgeon; 9. Charles Green, astronomer; 10. Dr. Daniel Solander, botanist; 11. John Ravenhill, sailmaker; 12. Antonio Ponto, seaman; 13. Drummer and marines; 14. Thomas Jordan and James Tunley, servants; 15. James Magra and Richard Littleboy, seamen; 16. John Satterley and George Novell, carpenter and carpenter's mate; 17. Thomas Hardman, boatswain's mate; 18. Thomas Knight, seaman; 19. John Gathrey, boatswain; 20. Richard Pickersgill, master's mate; 21. Alexander Simpson, seaman; 22. John Goodjohn, seaman; 23. Joseph Childs, seaman; 24. Thomas Mathews, servant; 25. John Woodworth, seaman; 26. Richard Hughes, seaman

14. 17. 18. 21. 23. 24. 25. 26.

15. 16. 19. 20. 22.

Barrels of rum and water

Spare sails

Seamen's chests

Hammocks

Across Australia

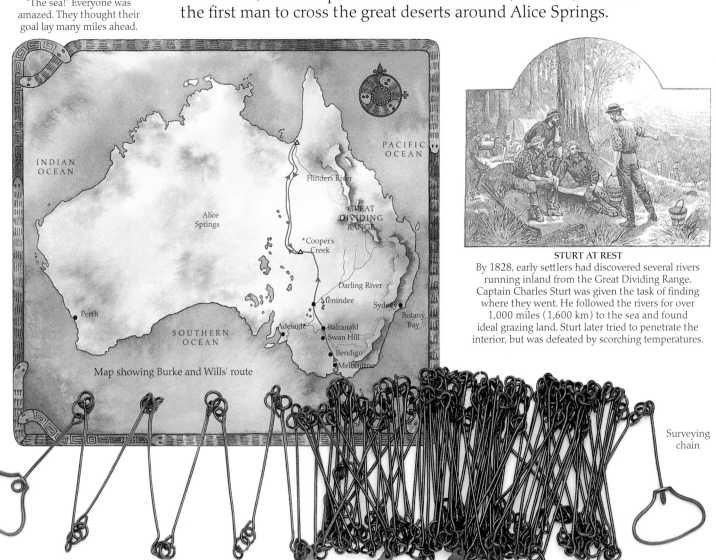

T HE FIRST EUROPEAN to land in Australia was the Dutchman Dirk Hartog, who touched on the west coast in 1616. However, it was not until James Cook's voyage (pp. 34–35), and later those of Matthew Flinders, that Europeans gained a clear idea of the extent of this vast continent. The first settlers arrived in Botany Bay in 1788. For many years, settlers were restricted to the coast, since no route over the Blue Mountains west of Sydney could be found. Then, in 1813, John Blaxland, William Lawson, and William Wentworth tried the novel approach of climbing the mountain ridges instead of following the valleys. In this way, they found a way over the mountains to the lush grazing land beyond. After this breakthrough, others attempted to penetrate the dry and lifeless interior, but some died on their travels. This fate was narrowly escaped by Peter Warburton, a retired police commissioner who, in 1873, became the first man to cross the great deserts around Alice Springs.

THE ULTIMATE PRICE
In 1860, Robert Burke and W. John Wills set out from Melbourne. They, too, like Stuart, were attempting to cross Australia. Supplies and men were left at Cooper's Creek, and Burke, Wills, and two others rode on ahead. They found the sea, but Burke and Wills died on the return journey.

"THE SEA!"
In 1862, John Stuart led a team north from Adelaide to find the northern coast. Suddenly, one of the men turned and shouted "The sea!" Everyone was amazed. They thought their goal lay many miles ahead.

Map showing Burke and Wills' route

INDIAN OCEAN
PACIFIC OCEAN
Flinders River
Alice Springs
GREAT DIVIDING RANGE
Cooper's Creek
Darling River
Menindee
Sydney
Perth
Adelaide
Balranald
Swan Hill
Bendigo
Melbourne
Botany Bay
SOUTHERN OCEAN

STURT AT REST
By 1828, early settlers had discovered several rivers running inland from the Great Dividing Range. Captain Charles Sturt was given the task of finding where they went. He followed the rivers for over 1,000 miles (1,600 km) to the sea and found ideal grazing land. Sturt later tried to penetrate the interior, but was defeated by scorching temperatures.

Surveying chain

FLINDERS' FLUTE
This flute belonged to Matthew Flinders (below). He may have played it during his long sea voyages.

MATTHEW FLINDERS
In 1798, the English naval officer Matthew Flinders was sent to explore Van Diemen's Land (now Tasmania)—which he sailed all the way around. Three years later, he sailed around Australia, charting much of the coastline and proving that it was one continuous land mass.

PASSING THE TIME
Mathew Flinders had this backgammon set with him on his long voyage around the coast of Australia. It was the custom for naval captains on long voyages to invite the ship's officers to social evenings, when they would play games such as this. Flinders was also accompanied by his cat, Trim, until the unfortunate animal went missing and was presumed dead on the French island of Mauritius in 1803.

BOX OF BELONGINGS
Flinders always made sure that his belongings fit into this wooden sea chest, which he took with him on his voyages. Space on board his ships was very limited, so he and his crew had to take as little as possible with them.

SURVEYING CHAIN
At the time Australia was being explored, surveying equipment was fairly primitive. Land was measured in "chains"—each of which was 66 ft (20 m) long—like this one (left) that dates from Flinders' time. When explorers found a suitable place for a harbor or a settlement, they surveyed it carefully for future use.

The Northwest Passage

ONE OF THE GREATEST GOALS of maritime explorers was to find the fabled Northwest Passage, a route from Europe to China around the north of North America (pp. 62–63). The more obvious routes around the south of South America and Africa were blocked during the 16th century by Spanish and Portuguese warships (pp. 20–21, 24–25). Several mariners explored the chilly, inhospitable northern waters, but they were all defeated by the extreme cold and strong winds. The search for the Northwest Passage was abandoned for a while, but then in 1817, the British government offered a prize of $50,000 to whomever found it. Many expeditions followed, the most tragic of which was that of Sir John Franklin in 1845, from which no one returned. Eventually, in 1906, Norwegian sailor Roald Amundsen (pp. 54–55) steamed through the Northwest Passage after a three-year journey.

FROZEN SEAS
On Dutch navigator Willem Barents's third attempt to find a northerly route to China (1595–97), ice pushed his ship out of the sea. His crew survived the winter, but Barents died on the return trip.

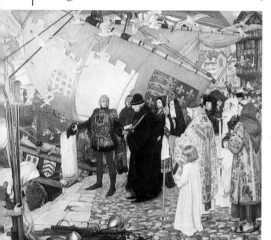

JOHN CABOT
In 1497, at the command of Henry VII, Italian-born John Cabot left Bristol in England to find a quick route to the Spice Islands off China's coast. He got as far as Newfoundland (pp. 62–63), which had already been discovered by the Vikings (pp. 12–13).

GIOVANNI DA VERRAZANO
In 1524, this Italian navigator found New York Bay and Narragansett Bay for the French. Here his boat is moored off what is now Newport, Rhode Island.

Handle is made from two pieces of bone riveted to outer side of blade

Bone handle is bound on with thong and gut

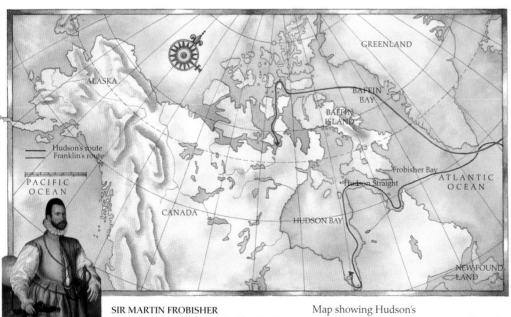

SIR MARTIN FROBISHER
In 1576, Queen Elizabeth I of England despatched Frobisher to find the Northwest Passage to China. He failed to do this, but he did discover Baffin Island, the bay of which is named after him. He returned home with what he thought was rock containing gold, but it turned out to be iron pyrites, now called "fool's gold."

Map showing Hudson's and Franklin's route

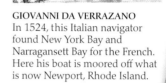

INUIT BONE KNIVES
These Inuit knives, found by one of the search parties sent to look for Franklin, are evidence of the tragic fate of his expedition. Local Inuit made the knives with scraps of steel from Franklin's abandoned ships. They attached the steel, which they sharpened to make a cutting edge, to handles made from bone.

Iron head   Bone   Wooden shaft

Copper head

Iron head

BOWS AND ARROWS
These weapons were found being used by Inuit hunters 10 years after Franklin's death. The arrowheads are made from supplies left by Franklin's expedition.

Inuit in canoe

HENRY HUDSON
In 1609, Henry Hudson (who had already made two voyages north from England) was employed by the Dutch East India Company to search for a Northeast Passage. He made one attempt, then sailed west in search of the Northwest Passage. In 1610, he set out again and discovered Hudson Strait and Hudson Bay. In June 1611, his crew mutinied. Hudson and eight others were set adrift and never heard of again.

SNOW GOGGLES
Arctic Sun shining on snow is dazzling and can cause temporary blindness. These leather goggles, which cut down the Sun's glare, belonged to Sir John Franklin.

GOURMET FOOD
This can of roast beef was found in 1958 near the last-known site of the Franklin Expedition, and was almost certainly part of their supplies. Cans like this were sealed with lead, which is thought to have caused some health problems. On an earlier trip to the Arctic, Franklin and his men had been reduced to eating "pieces of singed hide mixed with lichen, and the horns and bones of a dead deer fried with some old shoes"!

LAST MESSAGE
In 1859, the 14-year mystery of Franklin's fate was solved when this message was found by Captain Francis McClintock, who was searching for signs of the expedition at the request of Lady Franklin. The message was written in April 1848 by Lieutenant Gore, one of the expedition members, and recorded the death of Franklin, together with details of the plan to march overland to safety. None of the men on the expedition completed the journey.

One of Franklin's ships, *Terror*, stuck in ice

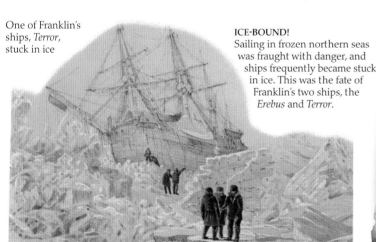

ICE-BOUND!
Sailing in frozen northern seas was fraught with danger, and ships frequently became stuck in ice. This was the fate of Franklin's two ships, the *Erebus* and *Terror*.

North America explored

WHILE CENTRAL AND SOUTH America were
being explored by gold-hungry Spaniards
(pp. 30–33), North America remained
virtually unexplored. It was not until the late 16th
and early 17th centuries that navigators such as
Henry Hudson (pp. 40–41), Jacques Cartier, and
Samuel de Champlain charted the eastern coast. English
and French settlers followed, establishing towns along
the east coast and along the St. Lawrence River. It was
from these colonies that trappers and frontiersmen
pushed inland. In 1803, the French emperor, Napoleon Bonaparte,
sold Louisiana to the United States for just $15,000,000. One year
later, President Thomas Jefferson sent Meriwether Lewis and
William Clark to explore and chart this newly acquired region.
Other journeys of exploration followed; gradually the vast interior
of the United States was surveyed and mapped.

ARROWS AND GUNS
While Samuel de Champlain was
exploring around the St. Lawrence
River in 1609, he befriended the local
Huron tribe. De Champlain joined
with them in a battle against the
Iroquois. The Hurons won—
their rivals were totally overcome
by de Champlain's guns.

TRAVELING LIGHT
Until the 18th century, the only
way into the interior of North
America was by river. Early
explorers traveled in canoes
made of birchbark stretched over
a wooden frame. These canoes
were light and easily controlled.

JACQUES CARTIER
In his search for the Northwest
Passage, French navigator
Jacques Cartier led three
voyages to the east coast
of North America. His
greatest discovery was
the St. Lawrence
River in 1534.
In 1536, Cartier
pushed upriver as
far as Montreal in
Canada, but could
go no farther by
water because
of the rapids.

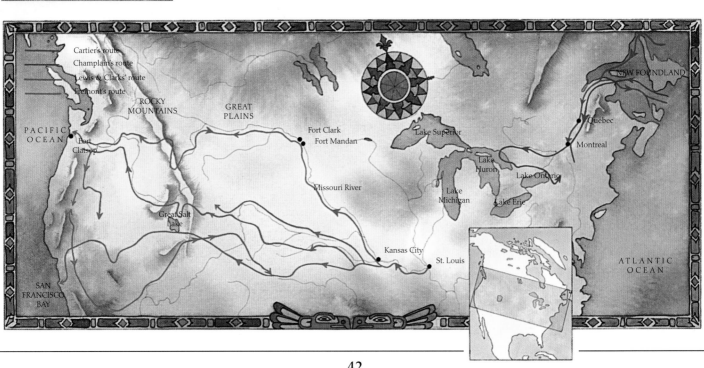

Cartier's route
Champlain's route
Lewis & Clarks' route
Fremont's route

ROCKY MOUNTAINS
GREAT PLAINS
PACIFIC OCEAN
Fort Clatsop
Fort Clark
Fort Mandan
Lake Superior
NEW FOUNDLAND
Quebec
Montreal
Lake Huron
Lake Ontario
Lake Michigan
Lake Erie
Missouri River
Great Salt Lake
Kansas City
St. Louis
ATLANTIC OCEAN
SAN FRANCISCO BAY

This token was worth one beaver skin

Many beavers fell prey to trappers because their fur was in demand.

TRADING MONEY
The Hudson's Bay Trading Company issued its own money—notes like this could be exchanged for English silver coins at its headquarters in London. Brass tokens were given to trappers and Indians in exchange for beaver skins. These could then be used to buy food and supplies from the Company.

Birchbark canoes like this were used by the now-extinct Beothuk tribe of Newfoundland

CLAIMING THE MISSISSIPPI
In April 1682, French trader and explorer Robert Cavelier, Sieur de la Salle, stood at the mouth of the mighty Mississippi River and claimed it for France. He also claimed the surrounding land, naming it Louisiana in honor of King Louis XIV.

RIVER ROUTES
French traders in search of furs acquired by local Indian tribes established routes into the interior along the Missouri River. Sometimes they took their pets with them!

Pointed blade with long cutting edge

BOWIE KNIFE
A good, stout hunting knife was essential to all settlers and frontiersmen. The Bowie knife—named after the American pioneer Jim Bowie—was one of the best. The stout blade could inflict deadly wounds and it was tough enough to cope with heavy-duty hunting work such as skinning.

This scalp belonged to a Native American from the Eastern Woodlands

HAIR-RAISING!
The Native American tribes encountered by North American explorers were almost always at war with each other. The scalp of an enemy killed in battle was one of their most important war trophies; the successful warrior would remove the skin and hair from the top of the victim's head. Sometimes they mounted the scalp on a wooden frame.

Continued on next page

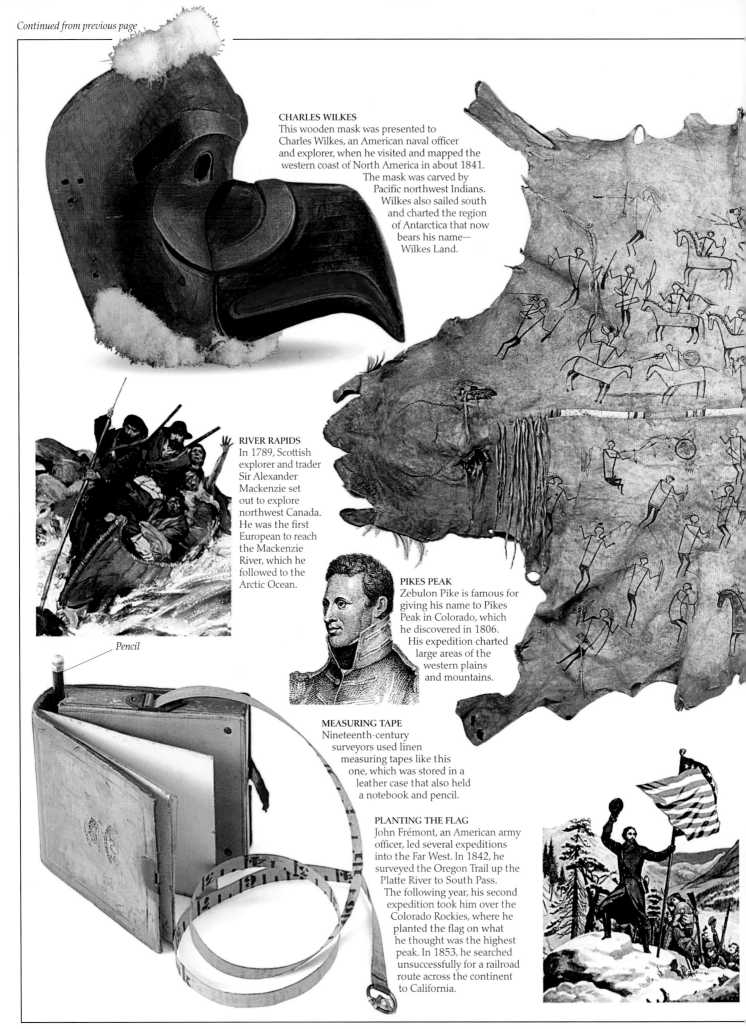

CHARLES WILKES
This wooden mask was presented to Charles Wilkes, an American naval officer and explorer, when he visited and mapped the western coast of North America in about 1841. The mask was carved by Pacific northwest Indians. Wilkes also sailed south and charted the region of Antarctica that now bears his name— Wilkes Land.

RIVER RAPIDS
In 1789, Scottish explorer and trader Sir Alexander Mackenzie set out to explore northwest Canada. He was the first European to reach the Mackenzie River, which he followed to the Arctic Ocean.

Pencil

PIKES PEAK
Zebulon Pike is famous for giving his name to Pikes Peak in Colorado, which he discovered in 1806. His expedition charted large areas of the western plains and mountains.

MEASURING TAPE
Nineteenth-century surveyors used linen measuring tapes like this one, which was stored in a leather case that also held a notebook and pencil.

PLANTING THE FLAG
John Frémont, an American army officer, led several expeditions into the Far West. In 1842, he surveyed the Oregon Trail up the Platte River to South Pass. The following year, his second expedition took him over the Colorado Rockies, where he planted the flag on what he thought was the highest peak. In 1853, he searched unsuccessfully for a railroad route across the continent to California.

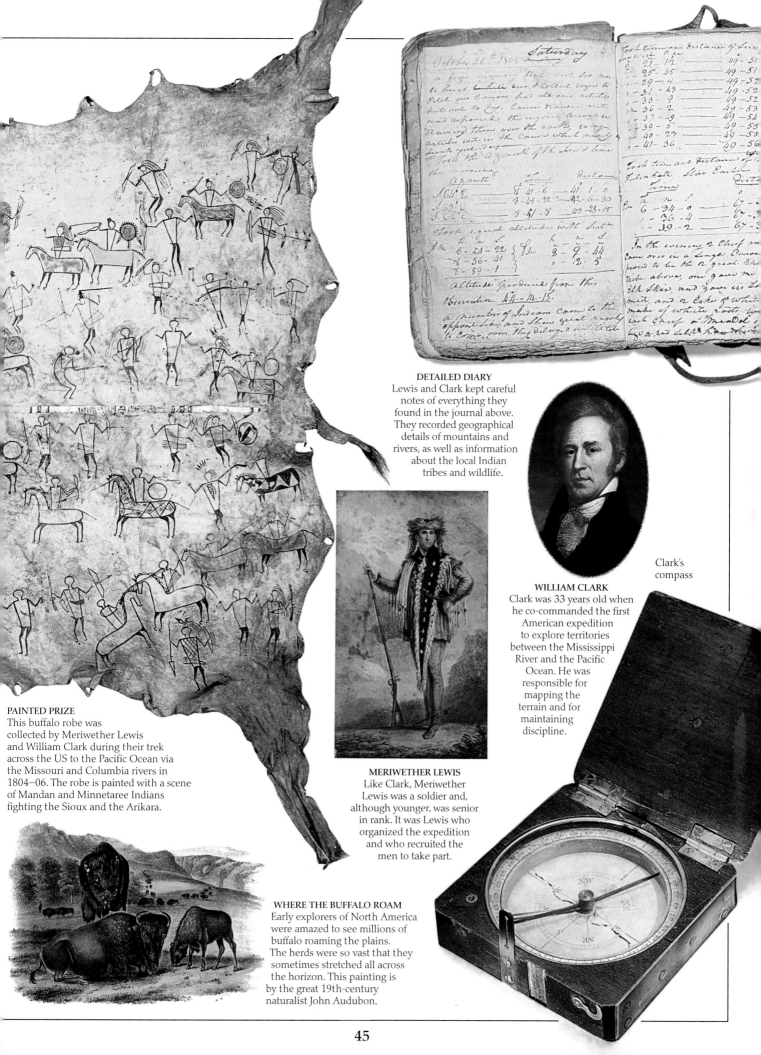

DETAILED DIARY
Lewis and Clark kept careful notes of everything they found in the journal above. They recorded geographical details of mountains and rivers, as well as information about the local Indian tribes and wildlife.

WILLIAM CLARK
Clark was 33 years old when he co-commanded the first American expedition to explore territories between the Mississippi River and the Pacific Ocean. He was responsible for mapping the terrain and for maintaining discipline.

Clark's compass

PAINTED PRIZE
This buffalo robe was collected by Meriwether Lewis and William Clark during their trek across the US to the Pacific Ocean via the Missouri and Columbia rivers in 1804–06. The robe is painted with a scene of Mandan and Minnetaree Indians fighting the Sioux and the Arikara.

MERIWETHER LEWIS
Like Clark, Meriwether Lewis was a soldier and, although younger, was senior in rank. It was Lewis who organized the expedition and who recruited the men to take part.

WHERE THE BUFFALO ROAM
Early explorers of North America were amazed to see millions of buffalo roaming the plains. The herds were so vast that they sometimes stretched all across the horizon. This painting is by the great 19th-century naturalist John Audubon.

The unknown continent

FOR MANY CENTURIES, Europeans knew little about Africa. While navigators were charting the oceans, and explorers traveled across the other continents, the African interior remained a blank on world maps—largely because it was such a dangerous place. Tropical diseases capable of killing a European within a day were common, and the jungles were full of lions, crocodiles, and African tribes who, threatened by the sudden invasion of strangers, could be aggressive and warlike. From about 1850, life became easier for explorers. Medicines to cure the most dangerous diseases were discovered, and modern guns could shoot animals and frighten tribal warriors. While some explorers followed the tropical rivers of central Africa to discover the great lakes—in particular, the Nile's source— others trekked the plains of southern Africa or explored deep into the jungle as missionaries.

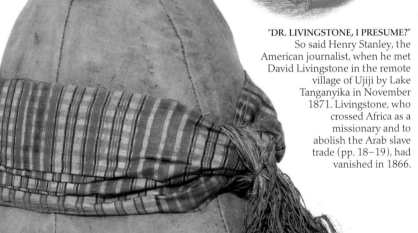

"DR. LIVINGSTONE, I PRESUME?"
So said Henry Stanley, the American journalist, when he met David Livingstone in the remote village of Ujiji by Lake Tanganyika in November 1871. Livingstone, who crossed Africa as a missionary and to abolish the Arab slave trade (pp. 18–19), had vanished in 1866.

JOHN HANNING SPEKE
Speke was an English explorer who made several journeys into central Africa. In 1858, he traveled with Burton to Lake Tanganyika, and then pushed on alone to discover Lake Victoria. In 1862, he went back to prove that the Nile flowed out of Lake Victoria.

AFRICAN WILDLIFE
Speke was also a fine naturalist. Wherever he went, he made notes and drawings of the wildlife and plants he saw. These sketches are of rhinoceroses.

SENSIBLE HEAD GEAR
This was the hat Stanley was wearing when he met Dr. Livingstone. Many early travelers in Africa wore these hats to protect themselves from sunstroke.

WHITE RHINOCEROS.

White rhinos are now threatened with extinction

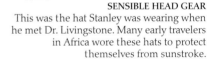

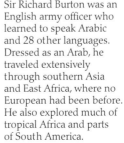

DRESSING THE PART
Sir Richard Burton was an English army officer who learned to speak Arabic and 28 other languages. Dressed as an Arab, he traveled extensively through southern Asia and East Africa, where no European had been before. He also explored much of tropical Africa and parts of South America.

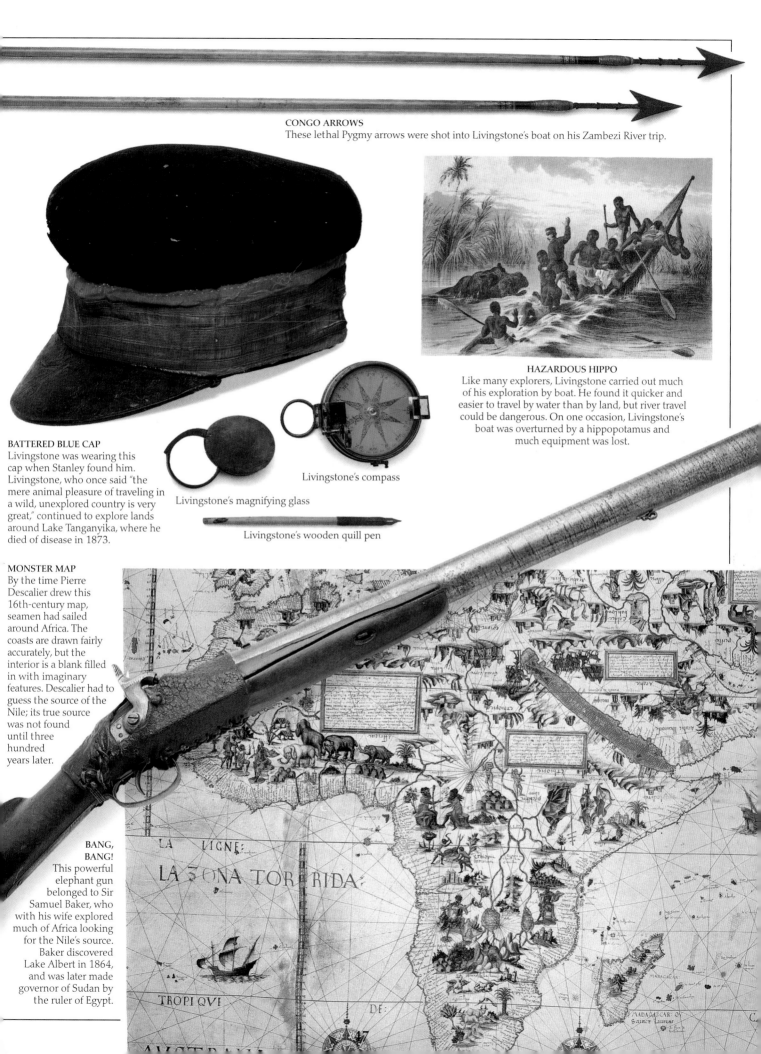

CONGO ARROWS
These lethal Pygmy arrows were shot into Livingstone's boat on his Zambezi River trip.

HAZARDOUS HIPPO
Like many explorers, Livingstone carried out much of his exploration by boat. He found it quicker and easier to travel by water than by land, but river travel could be dangerous. On one occasion, Livingstone's boat was overturned by a hippopotamus and much equipment was lost.

BATTERED BLUE CAP
Livingstone was wearing this cap when Stanley found him. Livingstone, who once said "the mere animal pleasure of traveling in a wild, unexplored country is very great," continued to explore lands around Lake Tanganyika, where he died of disease in 1873.

Livingstone's compass

Livingstone's magnifying glass

Livingstone's wooden quill pen

MONSTER MAP
By the time Pierre Descalier drew this 16th-century map, seamen had sailed around Africa. The coasts are drawn fairly accurately, but the interior is a blank filled in with imaginary features. Descalier had to guess the source of the Nile; its true source was not found until three hundred years later.

BANG, BANG!
This powerful elephant gun belonged to Sir Samuel Baker, who with his wife explored much of Africa looking for the Nile's source. Baker discovered Lake Albert in 1864, and was later made governor of Sudan by the ruler of Egypt.

LA LIGNE

LA ZONA TORRIDA

TROPIQVE

DE

Naturalist explorers

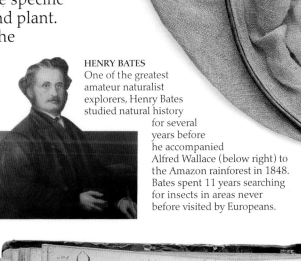

ALTHOUGH ADVENTURE OR PROFIT were the motives for many journeys of exploration, the thirst for scientific knowledge also became a powerful force in the late 18th and 19th centuries. It was a time when many naturalist explorers penetrated unknown territory with the specific purpose of discovering new species of animal, insect, and plant. Although earlier explorers had reported the details of the strange and wonderful wildlife they found, it was not until the late 18th century that naturalists began explorations with the sole goal of gathering scientific information. In addition to greatly enhancing our knowledge of the world, this activity could also bring great fame to those who were fortunate enough to discover new species.

An unusual way of collecting insects!

HENRY BATES
One of the greatest amateur naturalist explorers, Henry Bates studied natural history for several years before he accompanied Alfred Wallace (below right) to the Amazon rainforest in 1848. Bates spent 11 years searching for insects in areas never before visited by Europeans.

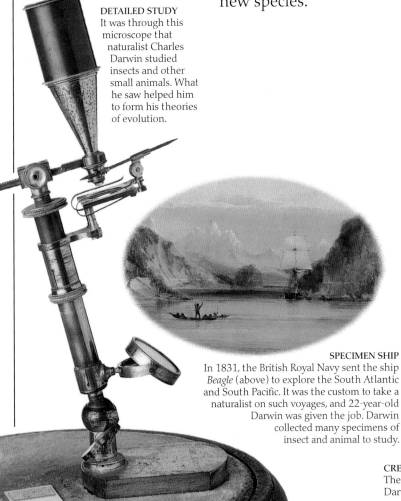

DETAILED STUDY
It was through this microscope that naturalist Charles Darwin studied insects and other small animals. What he saw helped him to form his theories of evolution.

SPECIMEN SHIP
In 1831, the British Royal Navy sent the ship *Beagle* (above) to explore the South Atlantic and South Pacific. It was the custom to take a naturalist on such voyages, and 22-year-old Darwin was given the job. Darwin collected many specimens of insect and animal to study.

CREEPY CRAWLIES
These are just a few of the beetles that Darwin collected on his journey.

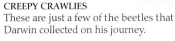

Brass
chloroform
bottle

Ivory-handled
pins

BANKS' BUTTERFLIES
Joseph Banks was a wealthy
amateur naturalist. In 1768,
he set sail with Captain
Cook (pp. 34–35). Cook
was under orders to explore the Pacific
Ocean, while Banks went to study the
animal and plant life. These butterflies
were among the large collection of
insects he brought back from Australia.

BOTTLE AND PINS
Insect collectors used chloroform
to kill specimens quickly and
painlessly. They
were then
pinned up for
detailed study.

**GENTLE
PRISON**
Naturalists used delicate nets
like this to capture insects. These
nets are so light that they do not
damage the delicate wings and
legs in any way.

MARY KINGSLEY
Nineteenth-century
Victorian England was
a time when most
respectable women
stayed at home—but
not Mary Kingsley!
She left her home
comforts to explore
West Africa in search
of new animals. Her
determination was much
respected by the men of
her time, and her work
was highly acclaimed.

FISH FETISH
By Mary Kingsley's time, actual
specimens were required to prove
that new species really did exist.
Mary was particularly interested
in fish. She preserved this
snoutfish in spirit and carefully
brought it back to Britain from
the Ogowe River in Africa.

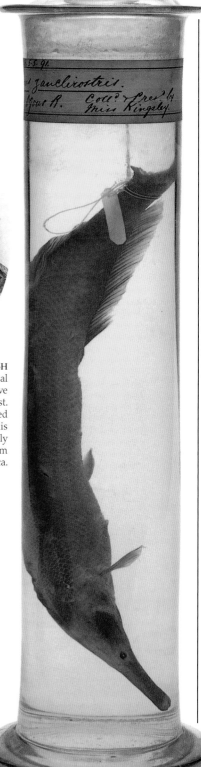

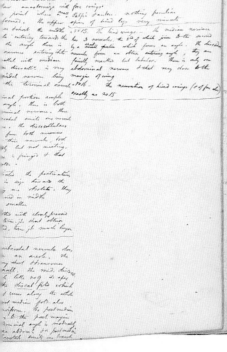

PERFECT PAGES
Henry Bates kept meticulous records of all
the insect species he found. The pages of
his notebooks, two of which are shown here,
are full of beautifully colored illustrations
and detailed written descriptions. During
his years in South America, he discovered
over 8,000 new insect species, 600 of
which were butterflies.

ALFRED WALLACE
Alfred Wallace traveled widely to discover new
species that he hoped would prove the theories of his
friend Charles Darwin. In 1848, he traveled to South
America with Henry Bates, and he stayed there for
four years. In 1854, he left Britain for Indonesia, and
remained there for the next eight years collecting new
insect species and exploring remote inland valleys.

Continued on next page

Plant collectors

The search for new plant species combines several of the most important ambitions of an explorer. By traveling to unknown regions in the hope of discovering new plants, botanist explorers (those who collect and study plants) combine the thrill of adventure with the excitement of scientific discovery. There is also money to be made from new plant discoveries, and many botanist explorers have become rich through their findings. However, the majority of 18th- and 19th-century botanist explorers were famous only in scientific circles. Today's naturalists campaign actively against the destruction of rainforests and the pollution of other habitats and are very much in the public eye.

HUMBOLDT AND BONPLAND
Alexander Humboldt and Aimé Bonpland traveled throughout South America during the early 19th century studying geology and collecting plants. This painting shows them seated among their instruments and specimens in a jungle camp.

Shoot from a *cinchona* plant

Cinchona bark from which quinine is obtained

MAGIC PLANT
Until the mid-19th century, malaria killed many people every year. During his travels with Humboldt in Peru (above), Bonpland collected samples of the *cinchona* plant. It was subsequently discovered that a substance obtained from the bark of the plant helped treat people who had caught malaria. The substance is quinine.

PRESSED PLANTS
These pressed eucalyptus leaves were brought back from Australia in the 19th century by Allan Cunningham. He later invented miniature glass houses that kept plants alive on long voyages.

Sarcococca hookeriana

BEARDED BOTANIST
Sir Joseph Hooker was a leading botanist explorer of the mid- to late-19th century. He took part in Sir James Ross's Antarctic expedition of 1839 and visited parts of Asia, where he collected many new specimens.

Hooker's satchel

Hevea brasiliense

Herbarium Mus

HOOKER'S BAG
Throughout his long travels, Sir Joseph Hooker wore this leather satchel into which he put any interesting plants he found. Several of the new species he discovered were named after him, such as the *Sarcococca hookeriana* shown here.

INTO THE JUNGLE
Naturalist explorers had to penetrate the most inaccessible areas in their quest for new plants.

Pressed eucalyptus leaves

This collection of notes is from Parry's first voyage to the Arctic

Arctic poppy

FLORA ARCTICA
These notes were written by Sir William Parry in the 19th century. Parry took part in five voyages of exploration to the Arctic between 1818 and 1827 (pp. 52–53), during which time he collected and studied vast numbers of plants. Parry's extensive records brought his explorations to the public eye.

Arctic moss

Pressed hibiscus

TYPE COLLECTION

BANKS' HIBISCUS
Sir Joseph Banks was the first great naturalist explorer. In 1768, he sailed with Captain Cook to the Pacific Ocean (pp. 34–35). He took with him two botanists, an astronomer, an artist, and four servants. Banks brought back this pressed hibiscus from Polynesia where its inner bark was used to make "grass" skirts (pp. 14–15).

Hibiscus tricuspis

RUBBER PLANT
The rubber plant was originally found by Spanish explorers of South America (pp. 30–33). Local tribes dried the sap of the plant to form bouncing balls that were used in games. This particular species, *Hevea brasiliense*, was discovered by the French scientist Charles Marie de La Condamine. During the 19th century, science found many new uses for rubber and demand for the plants soared.

51

The North Pole

THE HOSTILE AND DANGEROUS REGIONS of the Arctic (pp. 62–63) were the object of many 19th-century voyages. Explorations were led by naval officers instructed to map the remote regions and to report what they found. The expeditions sailed in bulky ships strong enough to withstand the pressure of ice and packed with enough supplies to last several years. The teams were equipped with many kinds of scientific instrument in order to collect rock samples and study wildlife. The men often went ashore on the bleak islands to continue their studies. The long series of expeditions culminated with Robert Peary's success in 1909. Peary was a US Navy officer who had already spent many years in the Arctic. In 1909, he led the first team of men to reach the North Pole.

POLAR PRIZE!
"The Pole at last!," wrote Peary in his diary. "My dream and goal for 20 years." In the late afternoon of April 6, 1909, Robert Peary and his team took the last steps of an agonizing trek to become the first men to reach the North Pole, a huge mass of ice that floats on the Arctic Ocean. The team consisted of his friend, Matthew Henson, and four Inuit companions—Ooqueah, Ootah, Egingwah, and Seegloo.

ARCTIC TRANSPORT
Polar explorers are faced with the task of shifting supplies and equipment across many miles of snow and ice. Sleds are used for this task. They need to be strong and big enough to carry heavy loads, but light enough to be hauled up slopes and moved by men and dogs.

SEALSKIN CLOTHING
Early Arctic explorers wore European-style woolen clothing, which failed to protect them from the Arctic elements. They later learned to wear clothing based on local Inuit designs. Sealskin hoods and mittens kept out the coldest winds and saved many an explorer from frostbite.

Tent poles

Sleeping tent for eight men

Tripod for ice saw

Rawhide

Iron-shod runners

Sealskin hood

Sealskin mitten

This Boat is left for Captain Parry and his party on their return from attempting to reach the North Pole.

It is particularly requested that she may not be removed, as they will probably be much in want of her.

H.M.Ship Hecla,
May 15th 1827

PLEASE DO NOT MOVE!
Before the days of radio communication, explorers were often out of touch for months at a time. In 1827, Sir William Parry and a team of men left their ship, the *Hecla,* to set out over land in an attempt to reach the North Pole. The team left this message on board a small boat, which was left behind for future use.

Tea kettle

RUM

Cooking utensils

Spirit lamp for cooking

SLED HAULING
Loaded sleds were very heavy to pull. The job was shared between teams of husky dogs and the men themselves.

Load protected by canvas cover

Net for carrying extra luggage

Pickax

Shovel for digging snow

The South Pole

CROSS-COUNTRY SKIS
Scott used these skis on his first expedition. They are 8 ft (2.5 m) long, wooden, and very heavy!

Wʜɪʟᴇ ᴍᴀɴʏ ᴇxᴘʟᴏʀᴇʀꜱ continued to be attracted to the Arctic regions, others turned their attention southward—to Antarctica (pp. 62–63), a vast continent where the climate is even harsher than that of the Arctic. Aside from the lure of being the first to reach the South Pole, there was a wealth of wildlife to study in the southern oceans, and the rocks of Antarctica were thought to contain fossils and minerals. Several British and Australian naval explorations of Antarctica culminated in the journeys of the two teams led by Captain Robert Scott. The first exploration team in 1901–04 gathered vast amounts of scientific data from the coast, while the second, in 1910–12, was designed to penetrate the interior. Scott led a team of five men to the South Pole, but was beaten by a Norwegian team led by Roald Amundsen (p. 40). After the Pole had been reached, the focus of exploration shifted to mapping and collecting scientific data. This work continues today.

THE RACE IS WON!
Roald Amundsen planted the Norwegian flag at the South Pole on December 14, 1911, a month before Captain Scott got there. He made the journey with four companions and 52 dogs.

Scott's mug from his first Antarctic voyage

Scott's shaving mirror

Scott's matchbox

SNUG AS A BUG
This caribou-skin sleeping bag belonged to the surgeon on Scott's second expedition. Some of the men slept with the fur inside, others with the fur outside. Whichever way it was used, the caribou skin was warmer than wool or sheepskin.

Scott's clasp knife

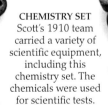

CHEMISTRY SET
Scott's 1910 team carried a variety of scientific equipment, including this chemistry set. The chemicals were used for scientific tests.

THE RACE IS LOST
The disappointed and exhausted Scott team reached the South Pole on January 17, 1912. On their desperate struggle back to base, Lawrence Oates, who was very weak and was holding up the team, said, "I am just going outside and may be some time." He walked out of the tent into the blizzard and was never seen again. Scott wrote in his journal, "We knew poor Oates was walking to his death." None of the team returned alive.

Oates   Scott   Evans
Bowers   Wilson

SIGHTSEEING
This telescope was used by Scott during his expeditions. It was a vital piece of equipment for the men attempting to navigate across vast frozen plains and through mountain passes, since it enabled them to locate the food and fuel caches previously left by the depot-laying parties. These were marked by small piles of stone with flags fluttering on them.

WINDPROOF HOOD
This hood was worn by the Irish explorer Sir Ernest Shackleton during his attempt to reach the South Pole in 1907–08. The extreme cold of the Antarctic winter made such clothing vital. Shackleton later signed the hood as a presentation gift.

FLYING FLAG
The American Richard Byrd mapped large areas of land and sea and was one of the first explorers to use aircraft (pp. 56–57). In 1926, he flew across the North Pole, and in 1929, he flew over the South Pole. He flew this flag from his aircraft as he crossed the poles.

BYRD'S PLANE
Richard Byrd's plane was called *Josephine*. You can see it here being unloaded from a ship in Spitzbergen (pp. 62–63).

Pioneers of the air

Hot-air and hydrogen balloons were the only way people could fly until the early 20th century. These balloons could not stay aloft for long and, since there was no way of steering them, they traveled with the wind. When the American Wright brothers made the first successful engine-powered flight in 1903, they heralded a new era of travel. Many of the early air pioneers were adventurous travelers who either flew across areas never before visited by humans, or who opened up air routes to previously isolated regions. Early aircraft were constructed from wood and fabric and were highly unreliable; many early explorers of the skies were killed when their aircraft broke apart or crashed. By the 1930s, aircraft were being used to map areas of land. Photographs taken from an aircraft accurately showed the layout of landscapes. Today, most maps are completed with the aid of aerial photography. It has even been possible to map inaccessible mountain areas.

BIRDMAN
This design for an artificial wing—based on a bird's wing—was drawn by Leonardo da Vinci, the great 16th-century Italian artist and scientist. However, the experiments were doomed to failure as human muscles are not strong enough to power such wings!

LADY OF THE SKIES
In the early 20th century, the world was amazed by the exploits of a young woman named Amy Johnson. In 1930, she flew solo from London to Australia in just 19 days, then a record. The following year, she flew to Japan over much previously unexplored territory.

Wooden spars to shape and strengthen wing

LIGHT POWER
Early engines were so heavy, it was difficult for aircraft to get off the ground! From 1908, new lightweight engines like this one were developed. The overhead valves, and light drive shaft and pistons gave it considerable power.

RECORD-BREAKER
Amelia Earhart set many records and outperformed many men. She vanished mysteriously over the Pacific in 1937, just before the outbreak of World War II.

AMELIA EARHART   LOCKHEED VEGA

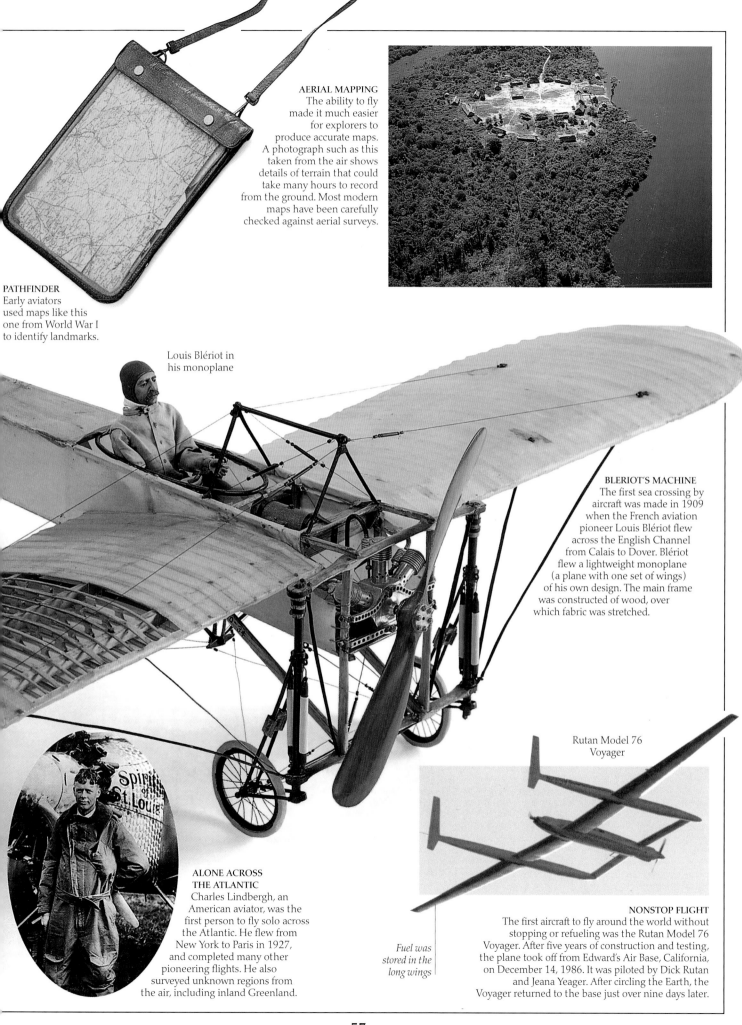

AERIAL MAPPING
The ability to fly made it much easier for explorers to produce accurate maps. A photograph such as this taken from the air shows details of terrain that could take many hours to record from the ground. Most modern maps have been carefully checked against aerial surveys.

PATHFINDER
Early aviators used maps like this one from World War I to identify landmarks.

Louis Blériot in his monoplane

BLERIOT'S MACHINE
The first sea crossing by aircraft was made in 1909 when the French aviation pioneer Louis Blériot flew across the English Channel from Calais to Dover. Blériot flew a lightweight monoplane (a plane with one set of wings) of his own design. The main frame was constructed of wood, over which fabric was stretched.

Rutan Model 76 Voyager

ALONE ACROSS THE ATLANTIC
Charles Lindbergh, an American aviator, was the first person to fly solo across the Atlantic. He flew from New York to Paris in 1927, and completed many other pioneering flights. He also surveyed unknown regions from the air, including inland Greenland.

Fuel was stored in the long wings

NONSTOP FLIGHT
The first aircraft to fly around the world without stopping or refueling was the Rutan Model 76 Voyager. After five years of construction and testing, the plane took off from Edward's Air Base, California, on December 14, 1986. It was piloted by Dick Rutan and Jeana Yeager. After circling the Earth, the Voyager returned to the base just over nine days later.

Into outer space

THE IDEA OF SPACE travel has fired people's imaginations for centuries, but the reality remained a dream until rockets powerful enough to lift objects into space were invented. Such rockets—developed by both the United States and the Soviet Union in the mid-20th century—were based on German missiles developed during World War II. The Space Age began in earnest in 1957, when the Soviet Union launched *Sputnik 1*, the first artificial satellite to orbit Earth—closely followed by the United States' space satellite *Explorer 1*. The next major step came in 1961, when a man orbited Earth for the first time. Another milestone in space exploration came in 1969, when American astronauts from the Apollo 11 mission became the first humans to land on the Moon. Today, exploration of the solar system involves sending robotic probes to investigate planets, asteroids, and comets, while Earth-bound and orbiting telescopes explore the universe beyond.

Capsule

Rocket

INTO SPACE
Years of work by the Soviet scientist Sergei Korolev resulted in a rocket that could carry a human into orbit. Yuri Gagarin was launched into space on April 12, 1961. His historic journey lasted less than two hours, during which time he completed one orbit of the Earth.

Rendezvous radar antenna

Docking tunnel

Lunar module, ascent stage

Control console

SPACE SPIDER
On July 20, 1969, Apollo 11's Neil Armstrong and Buzz Aldrin touched down on the Moon in their lunar module, just like the one shown in the image. They spent 300 hours there, during which time they collected rock samples, took photographs, and set up experiments. Television cameras sent back live pictures from the lunar surface. At the end of their mission, the module's ascent stage blasted off for the return to Earth, leaving the descent stage behind.

Fuel tank

Exit platform

Oxygen tank

Fuel tank

Lunar module, descent stage

Scientific experiments package

Landing pad

Lunar surface sensing probe

THE VOSTOK ROCKET
Yuri Gagarin was launched into space in a Vostok capsule some 8 ft (2.5 m) in diameter. A huge disposable rocket made up of four cone-shaped booster rockets attached to a central core rocket—and 13 times as big as the capsule—was necessary to launch him and the capsule into orbit.

Tomato soup

Chocolate pudding

Macaroni and cheese

Cherry drink

Dried bread cubes

MISSION FOOD
As soon as space flights began to last more than a few hours, the problem of food and drink had to be solved. To save weight, many space foods are freeze-dried or dehydrated (water removed). Astronauts use the water produced during the generating of electricity to rehydrate their meals. The food on the left came from US and Soviet space missions.

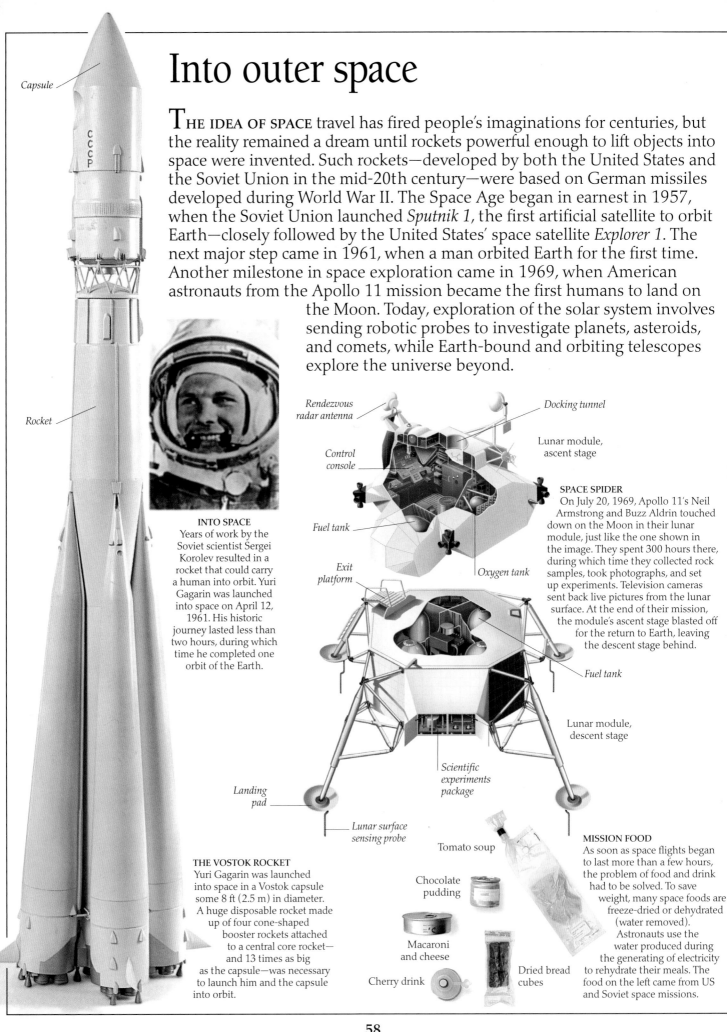

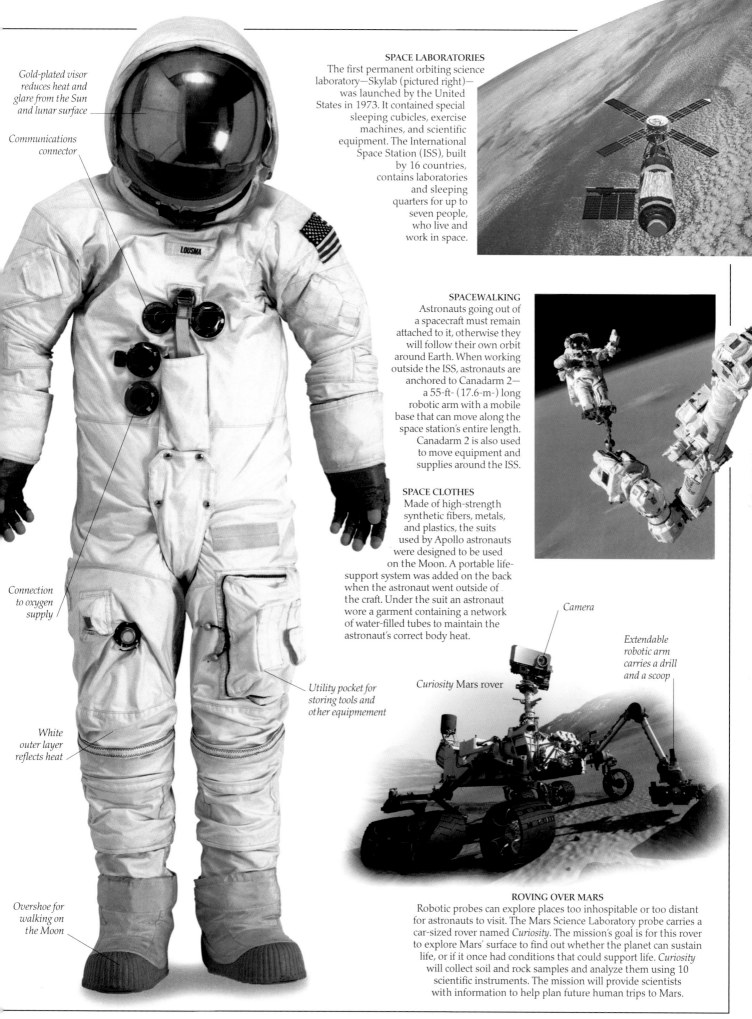

Gold-plated visor
reduces heat and
glare from the Sun
and lunar surface

Communications
connector

LOUSMA

Connection
to oxygen
supply

White
outer layer
reflects heat

Overshoe for
walking on
the Moon

Utility pocket for
storing tools and
other equipement

SPACE LABORATORIES
The first permanent orbiting science
laboratory—Skylab (pictured right)—
was launched by the United
States in 1973. It contained special
sleeping cubicles, exercise
machines, and scientific
equipment. The International
Space Station (ISS), built
by 16 countries,
contains laboratories
and sleeping
quarters for up to
seven people,
who live and
work in space.

SPACEWALKING
Astronauts going out of
a spacecraft must remain
attached to it, otherwise they
will follow their own orbit
around Earth. When working
outside the ISS, astronauts are
anchored to Canadarm 2—
a 55-ft- (17.6-m-) long
robotic arm with a mobile
base that can move along the
space station's entire length.
Canadarm 2 is also used
to move equipment and
supplies around the ISS.

SPACE CLOTHES
Made of high-strength
synthetic fibers, metals,
and plastics, the suits
used by Apollo astronauts
were designed to be used
on the Moon. A portable life-
support system was added on the back
when the astronaut went outside of
the craft. Under the suit an astronaut
wore a garment containing a network
of water-filled tubes to maintain the
astronaut's correct body heat.

Camera

Extendable
robotic arm
carries a drill
and a scoop

Curiosity Mars rover

ROVING OVER MARS
Robotic probes can explore places too inhospitable or too distant
for astronauts to visit. The Mars Science Laboratory probe carries a
car-sized rover named Curiosity. The mission's goal is for this rover
to explore Mars' surface to find out whether the planet can sustain
life, or if it once had conditions that could support life. Curiosity
will collect soil and rock samples and analyze them using 10
scientific instruments. The mission will provide scientists
with information to help plan future human trips to Mars.

Exploring the deep

NEARLY THREE-QUARTERS of the Earth's surface is covered by water, but it is only relatively recently that the mysterious world beneath the waves has been well explored. The first official expedition to investigate this underwater world was in 1872, when the ship *Challenger* was equipped with scientific instruments to gather information from the ocean depths. The introduction in the first half of the 20th century of "bathyscaphes," vehicles that could dive beneath the surface, was the next major development in underwater exploration. These enabled scientists to explore deeper than had previously been possible. As a result of the ever-increasing sophistication of diving vehicles and equipment, and the subsequent surge in underwater exploration, we now know that the lands beneath the oceans include mountain ranges, valleys, and plains similar to those we are familiar with on dry land.

Mermaids—mythical creatures that live beneath the ocean waves, half human and half fish—are said to attract men with their beauty and singing.

DIVING SHIP
Auguste Piccard and his son Jacques designed this bathyscaphe called *Trieste* to work at great depths. In 1960, Jacques took it down to 7 miles (11 km). The hull had to be very strong to withstand the pressure at such a great depth.

HEAVY AIR
Salvaging items from shipwrecks in shallow water has always been profitable. However, this activity used to be limited by the length of time a diver could hold his breath! In 1819, Augustus Siebe invented a copper diving helmet (left) that allowed divers to work at a depth of 200 ft (60 m) for long periods of time. The helmet was kept full of fresh air by a crew member on the surface who pumped air down a long pipe. The diver had to be careful not to damage the pipe, since this could cut off his air supply.

Helmet is made of copper and weighs approximately 20 lb (9 kg)

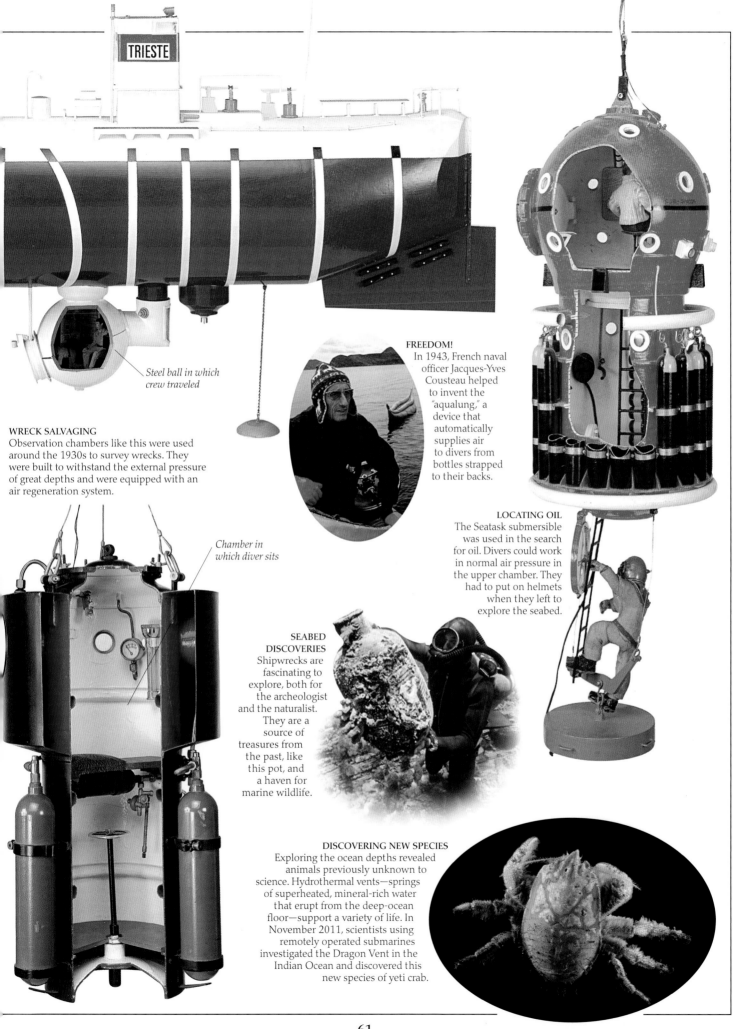

TRIESTE

Steel ball in which
crew traveled

WRECK SALVAGING
Observation chambers like this were used
around the 1930s to survey wrecks. They
were built to withstand the external pressure
of great depths and were equipped with an
air regeneration system.

FREEDOM!
In 1943, French naval
officer Jacques-Yves
Cousteau helped
to invent the
"aqualung," a
device that
automatically
supplies air
to divers from
bottles strapped
to their backs.

Chamber in
which diver sits

LOCATING OIL
The Seatask submersible
was used in the search
for oil. Divers could work
in normal air pressure in
the upper chamber. They
had to put on helmets
when they left to
explore the seabed.

**SEABED
DISCOVERIES**
Shipwrecks are
fascinating to
explore, both for
the archeologist
and the naturalist.
They are a
source of
treasures from
the past, like
this pot, and
a haven for
marine wildlife.

DISCOVERING NEW SPECIES
Exploring the ocean depths revealed
animals previously unknown to
science. Hydrothermal vents—springs
of superheated, mineral-rich water
that erupt from the deep-ocean
floor—support a variety of life. In
November 2011, scientists using
remotely operated submarines
investigated the Dragon Vent in the
Indian Ocean and discovered this
new species of yeti crab.

Exploration routes

THIS GLOBAL MAP shows the routes of some of the most important explorers mentioned in this book. As you can see, early explorers traveled only relatively short distances, but as technology improved, the intrepid men and women who followed in their footsteps were able to cover ever-larger areas. Many of them made detailed maps and notes of the areas they explored, and it is because of the information they gathered that we know so much about the world we live in.

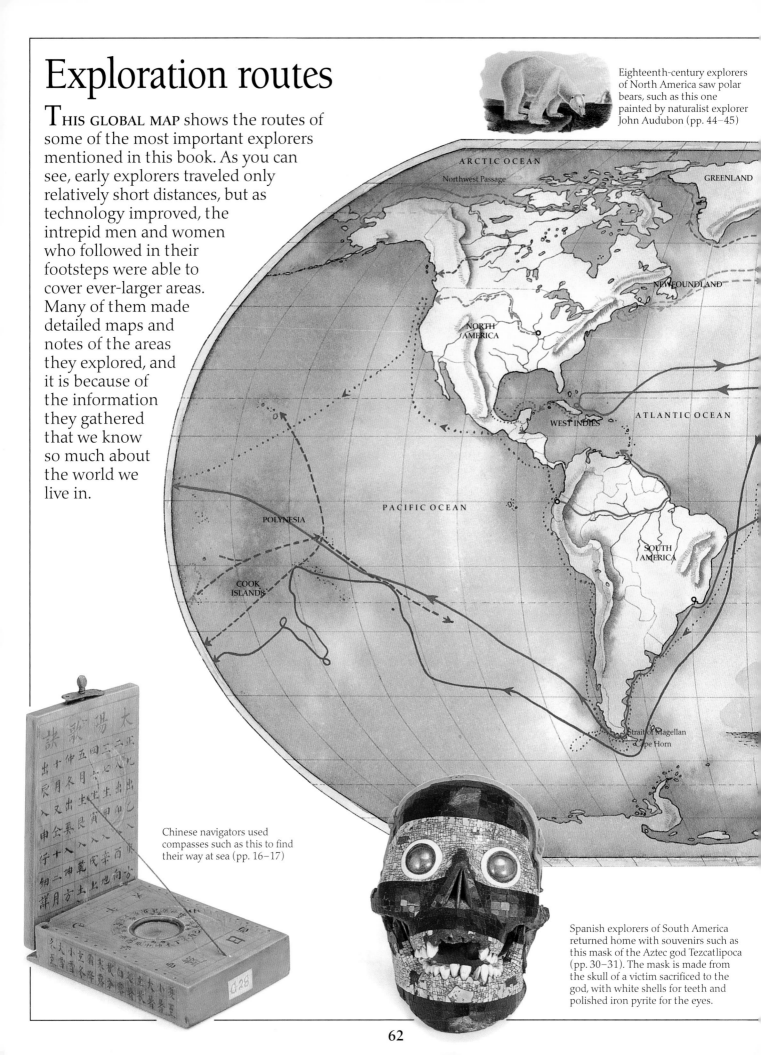

Eighteenth-century explorers of North America saw polar bears, such as this one painted by naturalist explorer John Audubon (pp. 44–45)

ARCTIC OCEAN

Northwest Passage

GREENLAND

NEWFOUNDLAND

NORTH AMERICA

ATLANTIC OCEAN

WEST INDIES

PACIFIC OCEAN

POLYNESIA

SOUTH AMERICA

COOK ISLANDS

Strait of Magellan
Cape Horn

Chinese navigators used compasses such as this to find their way at sea (pp. 16–17)

Spanish explorers of South America returned home with souvenirs such as this mask of the Aztec god Tezcatlipoca (pp. 30–31). The mask is made from the skull of a victim sacrificed to the god, with white shells for teeth and polished iron pyrite for the eyes.

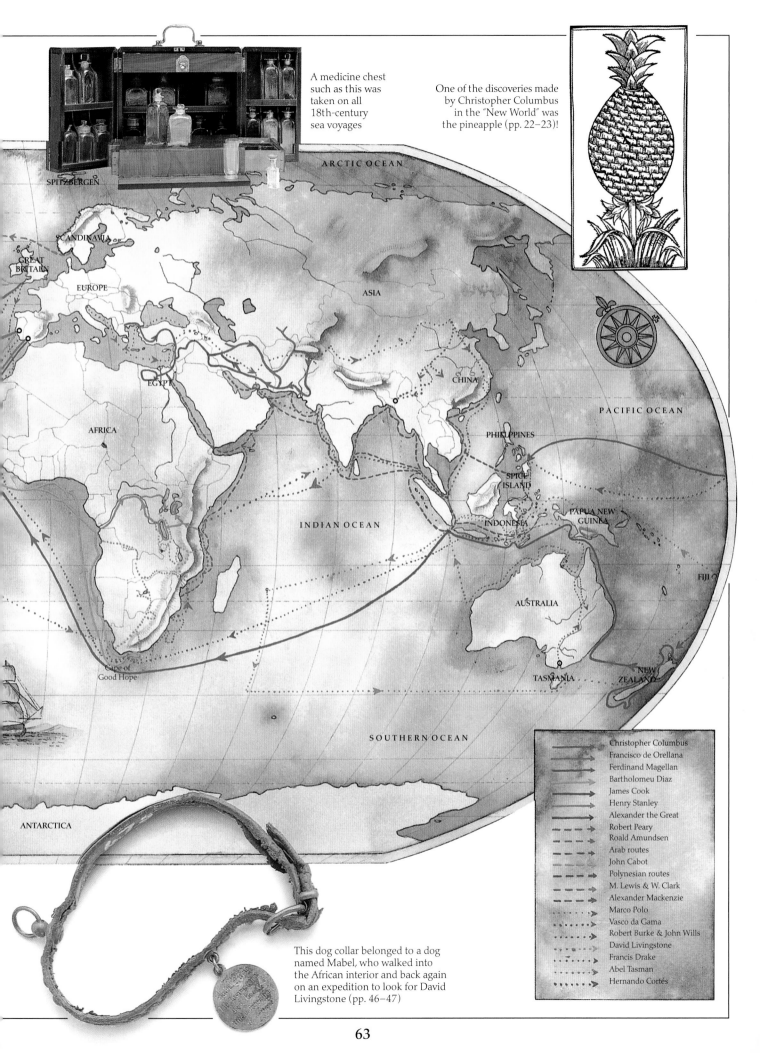

A medicine chest such as this was taken on all 18th-century sea voyages

One of the discoveries made by Christopher Columbus in the "New World" was the pineapple (pp. 22–23)!

ARCTIC OCEAN

SPITZBERGEN

SCANDINAVIA

GREAT BRITAIN

EUROPE

ASIA

EGYPT

CHINA

AFRICA

PACIFIC OCEAN

PHILIPPINES

SPICE ISLAND

INDONESIA

PAPUA NEW GUINEA

INDIAN OCEAN

FIJI

AUSTRALIA

Cape of Good Hope

TASMANIA

NEW ZEALAND

SOUTHERN OCEAN

ANTARCTICA

This dog collar belonged to a dog named Mabel, who walked into the African interior and back again on an expedition to look for David Livingstone (pp. 46–47)

Christopher Columbus
Francisco de Orellana
Ferdinand Magellan
Bartholomeu Diaz
James Cook
Henry Stanley
Alexander the Great
Robert Peary
Roald Amundsen
Arab routes
John Cabot
Polynesian routes
M. Lewis & W. Clark
Alexander Mackenzie
Marco Polo
Vasco da Gama
Robert Burke & John Wills
David Livingstone
Francis Drake
Abel Tasman
Hernando Cortés

Did you know?

AMAMZING FACTS

Early explorers had to face terrifying myths and legends, such as stories of huge sea monsters that swam in uncharted waters (probaby based on whale sightings).

In the 1400s, some Portuguese sailors who set out to explore the coast of Africa believed that the sea would boil as they neared the equator.

Sea monster on 1619 map

The Norwegian Viking explorer, Floki Vilgerdarson (later nicknamed Raven-Floki) carried three ravens (sacred to the Viking god Odin) on board his ship to guide him. Each time he released a bird, it returned to the ship. Then, one day, a raven flew forward. Floki followed it and discovered the coast of Iceland.

After Bartolomeu Diaz sailed around the southern tip of Africa in 1488, he called it "Cabo Tormentoso," or the Cape of Storms. The point was renamed "Cabo da Boa Esperanca" (the Cape of Good Hope) by King John II of Portugal.

On his voyage of 1497–98, Vasco da Gama's ships carried large stone crosses called padroes, which were positioned on high land near the sea.

Amerigo Vespucci, the Italian trader and navigator, not only gave his name to America, but he was also the first to use the phrase "Mundus Novus," or "New World," in a letter about the discovery.

When Columbus sailed across the Atlantic in 1492, he believed he had reached islands off Japan and China and called them the "Indies," the old European name for Asia. He died believing he had been the first European to find a westerly route to Asia, not the first to reach America.

Newly claimed lands were often named after their royal patrons, so the English colony of Virginia in North America was named in honor of Queen Elizabeth I, the Virgin Queen, and Louisiana for the French king, Louis XIV.

After Cortés had decided to invade the Aztec Empire with a force of just 508 soldiers and 100 sailors, he burned his ships so there was no turning back. His men would see victory—or death.

Banksia serrata, gathered from Botany Bay, Australia, on Captain Cook's first voyage

French newspaper cartoon of Peary's dispute

Magellan's ships were the first European ships to sail into the Pacific Ocean. However, Vasco de Balboa was the first European to see the Pacific, after crossing Central America on foot from east to west in 1513.

Balboa called the Pacific "Great South Sea" but Magellan named it "Pacific" because of its peaceful winds.

Naturalists on Cook's voyage to the Pacific in 1768 collected so many specimens in one bay in Australia that Cook named it Botany Bay.

Cook's reports of rich sea life in the unexplored Southern Ocean in the early 1770s attracted hundreds of sealers and whalers to the area, who almost hunted fur seals and the southern right whale to extinction.

Although linked as a pair of famous explorers, Henry Stanley and David Livingstone met only once and spent just a few months together.

European explorers in Africa did not travel light. Many had over 50 African porters to carry their equipment.

After Robert Peary returned from the Arctic in 1909, he was furious to learn that Frederick Cook was claiming he had reached it a year earlier. The US Congress later backed Peary's claim.

One of Vascco da Gama's padroes at Malindi, Kenya, used to claim land for Portugal

QUESTIONS AND ANSWERS

Q Who first crossed the Atlantic?

A For many years, people believed Columbus was the first to make the voyage, in 1492, when he sighted one of the islands of the present-day Bahamas, naming it San Salvador. However, there is evidence to prove that the journey was made around 500 years earlier by the Vikings. Settler Bjarni Herjolfsson is said to have sighted the coast of Labrador in 985, when drifting off course on route to Greenland. Leif Erikson, another Viking, became North America's first recorded European explorer when he set foot on the east coast of North America 15 years later, in 1000. Erikson named the land that he discovered "Vinland."

Q How did early explorers sail without instruments of navigation?

A Before the invention of instruments of navigation, explorers sailed by intelligent guesswork, using their knowledge of winds and ocean currents to estimate distance and direction. In unknown waters, clues such as driftwood and spotting certain seabirds suggested land was close. For example, the frigate bird does not land on water, so seeing one told sailors they must be nearing land.

Q Who discovered the secret of latitude?

A Latitude (north-south position) was first measured by ancient Greek scientists in the 3rd century BCE, using a scaphe, or hollow sundial. The Greeks also invented the astrolabe and Greek geographers were the first to draw lines of latitude on maps.

Q Why was the discovery of longitude so important?

A Although early seafarers could find their latitude from the Sun and stars, they had to use dead reckoning (keeping records of the distance and direction traveled each day) to figure out their longitude, or east-west position. Since it was easy to make mistakes, voyages were potentially dangerous and mapping inaccurate. By the time James Cook went on his second voyage in 1772, however, he could find his longitude with a highly accurate clock called a chronometer, which had been designed by the ingenious clockmaker John Harrison just a few years before.

Himalayas in central Asia

Q Why was the African interior unexplored by Europeans for so long?

A Mainly because it was dangerous! Tropical disease could kill a European within a day. There were savage wild animals, such as lions and crocodiles, and explorers had to contend with a variety of unknown landscapes from empty desert to swamps and thick rainforests.

Q Were all explorers' tales true?

A It must have been tempting for some explorers to elaborate tales of strange places. Although many did not believe Marco Polo when he spoke of Eastern springs that gushed black oil, he was, in fact, describing the Baku oilfields in modern-day Azerbaijan.

Frigate bird

Q Is there anywhere on Earth left to explore?

A Today, there is almost no place left on Earth still unknown and unnamed. We know what lies at the top of the highest mountains and, for the most part, in the ocean's deepest depths. As distant places become more familiar, the nature of exploration has changed. Rather than seek out the world's wild places, the challenge for explorers today is more to try to understand the Earth and preserve its wonders for future generations.

Record Breakers

 FIRST TO SAIL AROUND AFRICA
The Phoenicians are thought to have sailed around the tip of Africa from Egypt via the Red Sea on behalf of the Egyptian pharaoh, Neco (610–595 BCE).

 FIRST EUROPEAN TO SAIL AROUND AFRICA
Bartolomeu Diaz sailed around the southern tip of Africa in 1488 after a fierce storm drove his ships out of sight of land.

 FIRST TO SAIL AROUND THE WORLD
Ferdinand Magellan's expedition to find a westward route to Asia ended with one of five ships, the *Vittoria*, returning to Spain.

 LONGEST TRANSCONTINENTAL JOURNEY
This was made by Meriwether Lewis and William Clark from 1804–06, across North America to the Pacific Ocean.

 FIRST EUROPEAN TO FIND THE SOURCE OF THE NILE
John Harming Speke discovered Lake Victoria in 1858, believing it to be the source of the Nile. Returning in 1862 with James Grant, he discovered the point at which the Nile flowed out of the lake.

 FIRST TO SAIL THE NORTHWEST PASSAGE
The Norwegian explorer Roald Amundsen was the first person to navigate the Northwest Passage, sailing it from east to west from 1902–06.

 FIRST TO REACH THE NORTH POLE
Robert Peary made eight Arctic voyages, reaching the North Pole on April 6, 1909. However, many people still dispute his claim.

 FIRST TO REACH THE SOUTH POLE
Roald Amundsen reached the South Pole in December 1911, one month ahead of Captain Scott.

Timeline of exploration

In the past, explorers traveled to distant, unknown lands because of trade, conquest, and settlement. Today's explorers, however, are often inspired by adventure or scientific research. Some explorers, such as the Polynesians who sailed across the Pacific, are little known to us because they left no written records of their journeys. The entries below describe some of the world's great explorers and their remarkable achievements.

Christopher Columbus

c. 500 BCE HANNO
Phoenician; sailed from Carthage down the coast of West Africa and up the Senegal River looking for suitable sites for Phoenician colonies.

399–414 CE FA HSIEN
Chinese Buddhist monk; traveled across Asia on the Silk Road into India and across the sea to Sri Lanka.

629–54 CE HSÜAN TSANG (XUAN ZANG)
Chinese Buddhist monk; followed Fa Hsien's route.

800–1100 VIKING TRAVELERS
Crossed the North Atlantic; started settlements in Greenland (Erik the Red) and on the eastern coast of America (Erik's son, Leif Erikson).

1260–71 POLO BROTHERS, NICCOLO AND MAFFEO, AND NICCOLO'S SON, MARCO
Venetian; traveled across Asia to China. Marco Polo remained in China for almost 20 years, working for the Chinese emperor, Kublai Khan.

1324–53 IBN BATTUTA
North African (from Tangier); traveled through the Sahara to Mali and Timbuktu, in the Middle East and Arabia, and also visited India, Sumatra, and China.

1487–88 BARTOLEMEU DIAZ
Portuguese; sailed down the West African coast past the Cape of Good Hope, and entered the Indian Ocean.

1492–1504 CHRISTOPHER COLUMBUS
Italian; sailed across the Atlantic to the West Indies and, on later voyages, to the coasts of Central and South America.

1497–98 JOHN CABOT
Italian, backed by English merchants; reached Newfoundland and the American mainland in search of the Northwest Passage.

1497–98 VASCO DA GAMA
Portuguese; sailed down the West African coast, around the Cape of Good Hope, and across the Indian Ocean to India.

1519–22 FERDINAND MAGELLAN
Portuguese, backed by Spain; set off to reach the Spice Islands with five ships—one returned after circumnavigating the globe; Magellan himself was killed in the Philippines in 1521.

1519–21 HERNANDO CORTÉS
Spanish; conquered the Aztec Empire for Spain.

1531–33 FRANCISCO PIZARRO
Spanish; conquered the Incan Empire for Spain.

1534–42 JACQUES CARTIER
French; made three voyages of discovery to North America searching for a western route to Asia.

1576 MARTIN FROBISHER
English; reached Baffin Island in search of the Northwest Passage.

1577–80 FRANCIS DRAKE
English; circumnavigated the globe in his ship the *Golden Hinde*, plundering Spanish ships along the way.

1594–97 WILLEM BARENTS
Dutch explorer; reached the Kara Sea in search of the Northeast Passage.

1603–15 SAMUEL DE CHAMPLAIN
French; founder of French Canada who mapped much of the country's interior.

1607–11 HENRY HUDSON
English; made four voyages searching for both a northeast and northwest passage to Asia; discovered the Hudson River and Hudson Bay, where he died after his crew mutinied and cast him adrift.

1612–16 WILLIAM BAFFIN
English navigator; discovered Baffin Bay, Ellesmere Island, and Baffin Island.

1642–44 ABEL JANSZOON TASMAN
Dutch; sailed from Mauritius in the Indian Ocean to Tasmania, New Zealand, Fiji, New Guinea, then went on to Papua New Guinea and Java.

1678–80 ROBERT CAVELIER, SIEUR DE LA SALLE
French; explored the Great Lakes of North America and sailed down the Mississippi River to the Gulf of Mexico. Died trying to find the Mississippi delta from the sea.

Charles de la Condamine

Louis Bougainville

1725–29, 1734–41 Vitus Bering
Danish, appointed by the czar of Russia; crossed Asia by land to discover whether Russia and America were joined.

1766–69 Louis de Bougainville
French; sailed from the Falklands across the Pacific to the Great Barrier Reef on the coast of Australia, then to Java; first French explorer to sail around the world.

1768–79 James Cook
English; made three voyages around the Pacific, extensively mapping the southern Pacific and its islands.

1795–97, 1805–06 Mungo Park
Scottish; reached the Niger River in West Africa and later explored it upstream.

Henry Morton Stanley

1799–1804 Alexander von Humboldt
German naturalist; explored northwest South America.

1804–06 Meriwether Lewis and William Clark
American; sent by US President Thomas Jefferson to find a route westward from St. Louis to the Pacific Ocean. Their route took them along the Missouri, Yellowstone, and Columbia rivers by canoe.

1819–27 William Parry
English; commanded five expeditions to the Arctic, discovering part of the Northwest Passage.

1827–28 René Caillié
French; explored region surrounding the Sahara in West Africa; first European to visit Timbuktu and survive.

1831–35 Charles Darwin
English; explored South America and the Galápagos Islands, where he gathered information that formed his theory of evolution by natural selection.

Ranulph Fiennes

1839 James Clark Ross
English; explored Antarctic coast and ice sheets by ship, also searched for John Franklin (see below).

1828–30, 1844–45 Charles Sturt
English; mapped the Murray and Darling rivers and explored central Australia.

1840–41 Edward Eyre
English; found land route along the south coast of Australia from Adelaide to Albany.

1841–73 David Livingstone
Scottish; made four expeditions into Africa, crossing southern Africa and traveling south to Cape Town and Port Elizabeth.

1844–45, 1850–55 Heinrich Barth
German; traveled in West Africa and across the Sahara Desert.

1845–47 John Franklin
English; disappeared on his third voyage searching for the Northwest Passage.

1854–57 Richard Francis Burton
English; traveled with Speke in search of the source of the Nile River.

1854–1860 John Hanning Speke
English; discovered Lake Victoria in 1858, then the source of the Nile in 1860.

1860–61 Robert o'Hara Burke
Irish; traveled to northern Australia from Melbourne; died of starvation on the return journey.

1861–61 John Stuart
Scottish; crossed Australia from south to north, from Adelaide to Darwin.

1871–89 Henry Morton Stanley
American; made three expeditions across Africa and up the Congo River in central Africa; finding the "missing" Scottish explorer and missionary, David Livingstone.

1888, 1894–96 Fridtjof Nansen
Norwegian; made first crossing of Greenland cap-ice; deliberately allowed his ship to become frozen in the pack ice and then drifted across the Arctic Ocean, proving the existence of Arctic currents.

1907–09 Ernest Shackleton
Irish; traveled to within 100 miles (160 km) of the South Pole.

1908–09 Robert Peary
American; claimed to reach the North Pole after eight expeditions to the Arctic. Even though the US Congress backed his claim, many doubt that Peary reached the pole.

1910–12 Roald Amundsen
Norwegian; first to sail the Northwest Passage; first to reach the South Pole, using sleds pulled by dogs.

1910–13 Robert Falcon Scott
English; just beaten to the South Pole by Amundsen. The five-man team died on the return journey.

1943 Jacques-Yves Cousteau
French ocean explorer; helped invent the aqualung in 1943; he later assisted Auguste Piccard in developing the bathyscaphe.

1960 Jacques Piccard
Swiss undersea explorer; along with Don Walsh made the deepest-ever manned dive almost 7 miles (11 km) into the Mariana Trench in the Pacific Ocean, in the *Trieste*.

1961 Yuri Gagarin
Soviet cosmonaut; the first man in space.

1963 Valentina Tereshkova
Soviet cosmonaut; first woman in space.

1965 Aleksei Leonov
Soviet cosmonaut; first person to "walk" in space.

1968–69 Wally Herbert
British; led first dog-sled journey across the Arctic Ocean via the North Pole.

1969 Neil Armstrong
American astronaut; first man to set foot on the Moon, followed by Buzz Aldrin.

1977 Robert Ballard
American oceanographer and explorer; along with John Corliss, he discovered hydrothermal vents 8,200 ft (2,500 m) deep in the Pacific Ocean.

1992–93 Ranulph Fiennes
English; made the first unsupported crossing of Antarctica, with Mike Stroud.

Jacques Piccard

Find out more

T ODAY, LITTLE OF OUR WORLD remains unknown, and television brings faraway places into our homes. It is, therefore, difficult to imagine what it must have been like for the early explorers who did not know what they would find when they journeyed to distant lands. Look for television programs and movies that bring the journeys of various explorers to life. Check out your local museum to see if it has a specialized collection worth visiting, or use the internet to take a virtual tour of museums housing artifacts used by explorers.

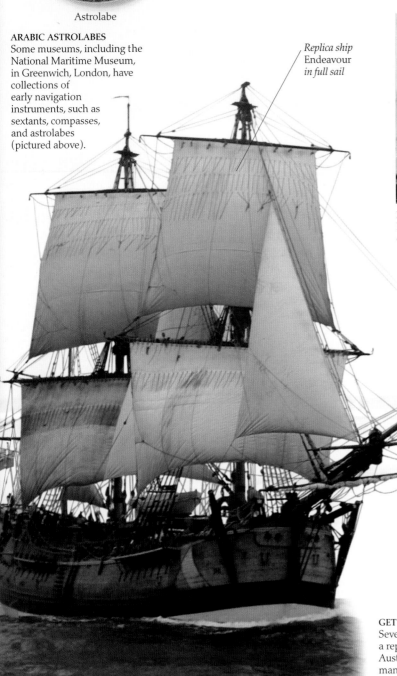

Astrolabe

ARABIC ASTROLABES
Some museums, including the National Maritime Museum, in Greenwich, London, have collections of early navigation instruments, such as sextants, compasses, and astrolabes (pictured above).

Replica ship Endeavour in full sail

PAINTINGS
Many art galleries and museums display portraits of some of the great explorers and paintings of their journeys. The painting above is by William Hodges, an artist on Captain James Cook's second voyage, and is called *Tahitian War Galleys in Matavai Bay, Tahiti* (1766). Look for dramatic photographs from more recent expeditions (including images sent back by space probes or pictures of newly discovered species taken by deep-sea exploration vessels), which are often printed in newspapers or shown on television news.

USEFUL WEBSITES

- Mariner's Museum (Newport, Virginia) home page with information on exploration, including biographies:
www.marinersmuseaum.org
- Site about Columbus's caravel, *Nina*, with information on building the replica and its sailing schedule:
www.thenina.com
- Interactive exhibit on Lewis and Clark's journey across America:
www.lewisandclarkexhibit.org
- To go on a virtual exploration of the world's oceans:
www.divediscover.whoi.edu
- Website devoted to the life and voyages of Captain Cook
www.captaincooksociety.com

GET ON BOARD
Several re-creations of sailing ships have been built. For example, a replica of Cook's ship, the *Endeavour*, was built at Fremantle in Australia between 1988 and 1994, following official plans and using many 18th-century methods. *Endeavour* normally resides at the Australian National Maritime Museum in Sydney, but it also sails to different Australian ports and other countries. In addition to touring the ship, you can even sail on it. Check out the website at www.endeavourvoyages.com.au for the latest information.

Sign marking the Lewis and Clark trail

WALK THE LEWIS AND CLARK TRAIL
You too can experience the epic journey made by Meriwether Lewis and William Clark across North America in 1804–06. Some of their route (which started at Camp DuBois in Illinois, then continued up the Missouri River, over the Rocky Mountains, down the Snake and Columbia rivers to the Pacific Ocean) can be walked on the Lewis and Clark National Historic Trail, which passes through 11 states in the United States. Log on to the website at www.lewisandclark.org to find out more.

DARWIN CENTRE
The Darwin Centre at the Natural History Museum in London houses 22 million preserved animal specimens. Visitors can tour 17 miles (27 km) of shelving, which holds glass vessels containing creatures collected from all over the world during the last 300 years. The collection includes snakes, baby crocodiles, and other finds collected during Captain Cook's first voyage to Australia in the 1770s.

Japanese experiment module

Centrifuge module

Photovoltaic array

Heat radiators

Truss structure

Crew return vehicle

International Space Station (ISS)

EXPLORE SPACE
Through the internet it is possible to link up to current voyages of space exploration. Browse the website http://spaceflight.nasa.gov/, which has information on all the latest NASA space missions. It even tells when you might be able to see the International Space Station (ISS) flying over a town or city and where you can watch a rocket launch if you are nearby. To learn of discoveries about the universe made by the Hubble Space Telescope and see the spectacular images it has taken, go to http://hubblesite.org/.

Places to visit

MARITIME MUSEUM OF SAN DIEGO, SAN DIEGO, CALIFORNIA
www.sdmaritime.com
This museum displays the *Star of India*, the world's oldest active ship; the *California*, a replica of a mid-19th century revenue cutter; and three other historic ships. Exhibits include the age of Sail, the Age of Stream, and Charting the Sea.

KENNDEY SPACE CENTER, CAPE CANAVERAL, FLORIDA
www.kennedyspacecenter.com
Visit the space center and see launch pads, rockets, historic technology, and real space hardware. Experience the excitement of the Apollo Moon program. Touch a real piece of Mars. There's even an interactive space flight simulator!

THE SANTA MARIA, COLUMBUS, OHIO
www.santamaria.org
In the city named after him, you'll find a life-sized replica of Christopher Columbus's flagship. Tours dramatize the daring of the explorer and his crew. An overnight program lets visitors sleep on board.

MISSOURI HISTORICAL SOCIETY ST. LOUIS, MISSOURI
www.mohistory.org
A great collection on Lewis and Clark's Corps of Discovery, including journals, maps, scientific specimens, and Indian artifacts.

NATIONAL MARITIME MUSEUM, GREENWICH, ENGLAND
www.nmm.ac.uk
This is the largest maritime museum in the world, with galleries dedicated to the history of exploration and how it shaped the world. There are also many paintings on display. Highlights include navigational instruments, such as James Cook's sextant and John Harrison's first marine timekeeper for finding longitude, as well as examples of atlases, maps, and charts, including a vellum Portuguese manuscript chart of the North Atlantic, created around 1535.

THE BRITISH MUSEUM, LONDON
www.britishmuseum.org/
The museum has thousands of objects from different cultures. Look for Chinese porcelain and jade in the China, South, and Southeast Asia gallery, as well as models of ships in the Egyptian galleries.

Glossary

ASTROLABE Navigational instrument used by the ancient Greeks and others to measure the height of the Sun or stars above the horizon; from the Greek words *astrer* (star) and *labin* (to take). (*see also* SEAMAN'S ASTROLABE)

BACKSTAFF Navigational instrument with a crossbar for sighting (like a cross-staff), and two circular arcs at either end. To take a measurement, the observer turned his back to the Sun, so the Sun's rays passed through the slot of the sight on the upper arc and hit the arc at the end of the rod. Invented by Captain John Davis in 1595 as a way of measuring latitude without risking the observer's eyesight by staring at the Sun. (*see also* CROSS-STAFF)

BALLAST Heavy material, such as concrete, stones, or lead, placed low down in a ship to increase its stability.

CARAVEL Small, light, three-masted ship usually rigged with lateen sails, designed by Portuguese shipbuilders in the 14th century; often known as the explorer's ship.

CARAVELLA REDONDA Caravel rigged with square sails. (*see also* CARAVEL)

CARRACK Northern European name for a type of ship known by Spanish and Portuguese as a Nao. (*see also* NAO)

CARTHAGE One of the most important Phoenician colonies, in North Africa (near present-day Tunis).

Dhow

CARTOGRAPHER Mapmaker.

CARTOGRAPHY The science and art of projecting part of the Earth's surface onto a flat plane.

CARTOUCHE Oval shape in which Egyptian characters representing a ruler's name were written.

CINCHONA Plant from which quinine is obtained; used by explorers to ease the symptoms of malaria.

COMPASS Instrument used by mariners to navigate in which a magnetized metal needle aligns itself with the Earth's magnetic fields; invented by the Chinese over 2,000 years ago. (*see also* LODESTONE)

CROSS-STAFF Simple navigational instrument to measure a ship's latitude. The navigator lined up the crossbar between the Sun or the North Star and the horizon, then read off the angle of the Sun or star from the horizon, enabling him to calculate the ship's distance from the equator. (*see also* BACKSTAFF)

DEAD RECKONING A navigational method based on keeping records of the distance and direction sailed from a known point, such as a port.

DHOW Sailing ship with triangular lateen sails rigged on one or two masts; used for hundreds of years by Muslim traders in the Persian Gulf and Indian Ocean.

EL DORADO Spanish for "The Golden One," or a ruler dusted with gold; came to mean a legendary city of gold, searched for by Spanish explorers and others in Central and South America.

ENDEAVOUR Captain James Cook's ship on his voyage to the Pacific in 1768–71. The *Endeavour* was a coal-carrier from Whitby, England, armed with six carriage guns and eight swivel guns with a large storage hold. The ship was broken up in 1793.

GOLDEN HINDE Francis Drake's ship on his circumnavigation of the globe (1577–80).

HARDTACK A type of cracker that lasted for years, often taken on long sea voyages.

JADE Hard, ornamental stone of varying colors, often green, prized in China, Mexico, and South America. Chinese carvings made of jade were often traded down the Silk Road. (*see also* SILK ROAD)

JUNK Large Chinese sailing ship with a flat bottom; usually used to carry cargo.

KNARR (or *KNORR*) Large, Viking ship that sat deeper in the water than a longship, used for carrying passengers and cargo. (*see also* LONGSHIP)

LATEEN-RIGGED Triangular sail(s) rigged on a short mast; named from the word "Latin" by Northern Europeans visiting the Mediterranean region.

LATITUDE Position to the north or south on Earth's surface, measured in degrees north or south of the equator. On a globe, latitude is shown in parallels (imaginary lines running east to west). (*see also* LONGITUDE)

LODESTONE Naturally magnetic iron oxide—used by early explorers when navigating at sea because of its north-pointing characteristic; discovered by the Chinese about 2,000 years ago. Lodestone was also used to magnetize compass needles. (*see also* COMPASS)

LOGBOOK A record of a ship's voyage kept by the captain, which usually included the ship's direction, speed, and distance traveled, and any events on board ship, such as sickness among the crew or sightings of land or other ships.

LONGITUDE Position to the east or west on the Earth's surface. On a globe, longitude is shown in meridians (imaginary lines running north to south), which divide Earth into 360 degrees. Longitude is measured in degrees east or west from a known starting point—the meridian running through Greenwich, England. Every 15 degrees of longitude is equal to one hour of time. (*see also* LATITUDE)

Cartographer

Jade carving

LONGSHIP Long, narrow Viking ship, often used by warriors on raids but also for long-distance travel. (*see also* KNARR)

MATCHLOCK Gun with an early, simple firing mechanism in which an S-shaped lever was pressed down to force a match (or lighted wick) into a flashpan, which ignited the powder. Used by early explorers; later replaced by the flintlock.

MORION HELMET Type of lightweight open helmet often made of a single piece of steel or two pieces joined at the top with a board brim and peak; popular in the mid-16th century with European soldiers.

MYRRH Valuable bitter aromatic gum from the bark of a tree, used in perfume, incense, medicines, and to anoint the dead; an important part of Egyptian religious ceremonies.

Santa Maria

NAO Large sailing ship, bigger bellied than a caravel, originally built as a merchant ship and used on many voyages of exploration to carry supplies and weapons; became the most popular European ship for trading, exploration and warfare in the 16th century until replaced by the galleon. Northern Europeans called this type of ship a carrack.

NINA One of the three ships on Columbus's first voyage of discovery, along with the *Pinta* and the *Santa Maria*. Columbus returned to Spain in the *Nina* after the *Santa Maria* was wrecked.

NORTH STAR A bright star almost at the north celestial pole (the point in the sky directly above the Earth's North Pole), used by early navigators in the northern hemisphere to work out their position at sea; also called Polaris or the North Star.

NORTHEAST PASSAGE Northern route from Europe to China through the Arctic. The first person to travel through it was the Norwegian Nils Nordenskjold, on a scientific expedition in 1878–79.

NORTHWEST PASSAGE Route through the Arctic seas along the coast of North America giving access to the East from Europe. It was finally navigated by Roald Amundsen, from 1903 to 1906.

PORCELAIN Hard, translucent pottery invented by the Chinese; much in demand in Europe.

QUADRANT An instrument for navigation shaped like a quarter circle with an attached plumbline (weighted string) used to determine the position of the Sun and stars. The navigator lined up one of the quadrant's straight sides with the Sun or the North Star, then read off the position of the plumbline to work out the ship's approximate latitude. (*see also* NORTH STAR)

SANTA MARIA A caravel from northern Spain and Columbus's flagship on his first voyage of discovery; wrecked off the West Indies in 1492. (*see also* CARAVEL)

SCURVY Often fatal disease caused by lack of vitamin C, which is found in fresh fruit and vegetables; formerly the leading cause of death among sailors on long sea voyages.

SEAMAN'S ASTROLABE Instrument used to calculate a ship's latitude; the navigator lined up a sighting rule at the center of a brass ring and used it to sight the Sun or a star then read off the angle from markings around the ring. (*see also* ASTROLABE)

SEXTANT Instrument of navigation invented in the 1700s as a more accurate way of measuring latitude than the cross-staff and backstaff. The navigator looked through a sighting tube and moved a bar until the Sun and horizon were lined up in small mirrors, then read off the angle.

SILK ROAD One of the world's oldest trade routes, which ran about 4,300 miles (7,000 km) across China and Asia; used by merchants from around 500 BCE for hundreds of years before gradually falling into decline.

Sextant

SPICE ISLANDS European name given to islands in the Indian Ocean, where valuable spices, such as cinnamon, originated.

SQUARE RIGGED A square sail suspended from a yard (a horizontal wooden beam) on a mast.

TIMBUKTU Important trading center just south of the Sahara Desert in Africa; the subject of many myths among Europeans.

VELLUM A kind of fine parchment prepared from the skin of calves, kids, or lambs dipped in lime-baths and burnished. Vellum was expensive, but held the ink better than ordinary hard parchment, so was good for seafaring charts, which needed to be rolled and rerolled many times. Ordinary parchment was used for bound material, such as logbooks. Vellum and parchment were more widely available than paper.

VITTORIA A carrack; one of the five ships on Magellan's voyage to discover a route to Asia from the west (the others were the *Conceptión*, the *San Antonio*, the *Santiago*, and the *Trinidad*). It was the only ship to complete the journey around the globe and home to Spain.

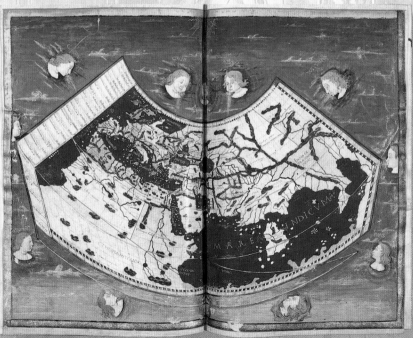

Map drawn on vellum

Index

A

Africa 11, 16, 17, 18, 19, 20, 21, 46–47, 49, 64, 65
Age of Exploration 20–25
Agnese, Battista 24
aircraft 55, 56–57
Alexander the Great 10, 63
Alvarado, Pedro de 30
Amazon rainforest 48
America, discovery of 22–23
Amundsen, Roald 40, 54, 63, 65, 67
animals 34, 45, 46, 47, 48–49, 61
Antarctica 44, 50, 54–55
Arabs 18–19, 63
Arctic 40–41, 44, 51, 52–53, 64, 65
Armstrong, Neil 58, 67
Asia 16–17
astrolabes 23, 29, 68, 70
astronauts 58–59
Atahualpa, King 32
Atlantic Ocean 13, 22–23, 24, 48, 65
Audobon, John 45, 62
Australia 17, 34, 38–39, 49, 50
Aztec Empire 23, 30–31, 33, 62, 64

B

backstaffs 28, 70
Baker, Sir Samuel 47
Banks, Sir Joseph 35, 49, 51
Barents, Willem 40, 66
Bates, Henry 48, 49
bathyscaphes 60–61
Blaxland, John 38
Blériot, Louis 57
Burke, Robert 38, 63, 67
Burton, Sir Richard 46, 67
Byrd, Richard 55

C

Cabot, John 40, 63, 66
Canada 40–41, 42, 44
canoes 14, 41, 42–43
Cape of Good Hope 20, 21, 24
Cape Horn 24
Carthaginians 6
Cartier, Jacques 42, 66
cartographers 34, 45, 57, 70
Cavelier, Robert, Sieur de la Salle 43, 66
cedar wood 9

Champlain, Samuel de 42, 66
Charles I of Spain 24
Cheng Ho 17
China 16–17, 18, 20, 40
Christianity 33
chronometers 28, 34
cinchona plant 50
circumnavigation of the world 24–25, 57, 65
Clark, William 42, 45, 63, 67, 69
clothing 27, 52–53, 55, 59
coal-carriers 36–37
coins 6, 7, 10, 11, 13, 16, 21, 23, 32
Columbus, Christopher 22–23, 24, 30, 63, 64, 65, 66
compasses 21, 29, 45, 47, 62, 70
conquistadors 30–33
Cook, Captain James 29, 34–37, 38, 49, 51, 63, 64, 67, 68, 69
Coronado, Francisco 33
Cortés, Hernando 23, 30, 31, 63, 64, 66
Cousteau, Jacques-Yves 61, 67
cross-staffs 28–29, 70
Cunningham, Allan 50

D

da Gama, Vasco 20, 63, 64, 66
Darwin, Charles 48, 49, 67
dead reckoning 28, 70
Descalier, Pierre 47
dhows 18–19, 70
Diaz, Bartolomeu 21, 63, 64, 65, 66
disease 46, 50
divers 60–61
dividers 25
Drake, Sir Francis 25, 63, 66

EF

Earhart, Amelia 56
Egyptians 8–9, 65
Elizabeth I 25, 40, 64
Endeavour, the 36–37, 68, 70
equator, crossing the 27
Erik the Red 12, 66
Ferdinand and Isabella of Spain 22, 23
Fiennes, Ranulph 67
Fiji 34, 35
flat Earth 8
Flinders, Matthew 38, 39
food 26, 27, 35, 41, 58
Franklin, Sir John 40–41, 67
Frémont, John 44
Frobisher, Sir Martin 40, 66

fruit and vegetables 22, 35, 63
fur trade 43

GH

Gagarin, Yuri 58, 67
globes 25
gold 13, 18, 23, 30, 32
Gomes, Fernao 21
Great South Sea 34–35
Greeks 10–11
Greenland 12, 13, 65
hammock 22, 26
Hartog, Dirk 38
Hatshepsut, Queen 8, 9
Hawaiian islands 34
Hedin, Sven 17
Henry the Navigator 20
Hooker, Sir Joseph 50
Hudson, Henry 40–41, 42, 66
Hudson Bay 41
human sacrifice 33
Humboldt, Alexander von 50, 67

I

Ibn Battuta 19, 66
Iceland 10
Inca Empire 30, 32, 33
India 10, 18, 20
Indian Ocean 18, 25, 61
Indians 30–33, 42–43, 45
Indonesia 18, 20, 49
Inuits 40–41, 52
Ireland 13
ivory 10, 18, 21

JK

Jason and the Argonauts 10
Johnson, Amy 56
junks 17, 70
Kingsley, Mary 49
knarrs 12–13, 70
Korolev, Sergei 58
Kublai Khan 17

LM

La Condamine, Charles Marie de 51
latitude 18, 65, 70
Lawson, William 38
Leif Erikson 12, 65, 66
Leonardo da Vinci 56
Lewis, Meriwether 42, 45, 63, 67, 69
Lindbergh, Charles 57
Livingstone, David 19, 46–47, 63, 64, 67
lodestone 28, 70
logbooks 29, 70
longitude 28, 34, 65, 70

longships 12–13, 71
McClintock, Captain Francis 41
Mackenzie, Sir Alexander 44, 63
Magellan, Ferdinand 24–25, 63, 64, 65, 66
maps 6, 22, 23, 24–25, 34, 45, 47, 57, 62–63
Mars 59
Mayan civilization 31
Mediterranean 6–7, 11
Mexico 30, 31
missionaries 46
Mississippi River 43, 45
Missouri River 43, 45
Moon landings 58
myrrh 9, 71

NO

Nansen, Fridtjof 67
naturalists 35, 45, 46, 48–51, 62, 64
nautical almanacs 28
navigational instruments 18, 21, 23, 24–25, 28–29, 54–55, 62, 65
New World 22–23, 30–33
New Zealand 34
Newfoundland 13, 40, 42
Nile River 8, 46, 47, 65
North America 12, 13, 32, 33, 34, 40–45
North Pole 52–53, 65
North Star 28, 29, 71
Northwest Passage 40–41, 65, 71
Oates, Lawrence 55
Oregon Trail 44

P

Pacific Ocean 14, 24, 25, 34–35, 45, 48, 51, 64
parallel rulers 24–25
Parry, Sir William 51, 53, 67
Peary, Robert 52, 63, 64, 65, 67
Persian Empire 10
Persian Gulf 17, 18
Peru 30, 50
Philippines 20
Phoenicians 6–7, 65
Piccard, Auguste and Jacques 60, 67
Pigafetta, Antonio 24
Pike, Zebulon 44
Pizzaro, Francisco 30, 32, 66
plant collectors 50–51
plunder 12, 13, 25
Polo, Marco 16, 17, 63, 65, 66
Polynesians 14–15, 35, 63
porcelain 16, 71
Portugal 20–21, 24–25, 64

pottery 6, 10–11, 16
priests 33
Przhevalsky, Nicolay 17
Punt 8, 9

QR

quadrants 18, 71
Raleigh, Sir Walter 22
religion 33
Rocky Mountains 44
Romans 10–11
rubber 51
Rutan Model 76 Voyager 57

S

sailmaker's tools 26
sailors
    Endeavour's crew 36–37
    life at sea 26–27, 39
St. Lawrence River 42
Santa Maria 23
satellites 28
Scott, Captain Robert 54–55, 65, 67
scrimshaw 26
scurvy 26, 35, 71
sea chests 26–27, 39
sea monsters 24, 64
settlers
    Polynesian 14–15
    Viking 12, 13
sextants 29, 71
Shackleton, Sir Ernest 55, 67
ships
    Arab dhows 18–19
    Chinese 17
    Egyptian 8–9
    Endeavour, the 36–37, 68
    Greek and Roman 10–11
    life at sea 26–27
    Phoenician 6–7
    Polynesian 14
    Portuguese and Spanish caravels 20–21, 23, 70
    Viking 12–13
shipwrecks 60, 61
Siebe, Augustus 60
Sierra Leone 20
silk 16, 18
Silk Road 16–17, 71
silver 11, 13, 32
Sinbad the Sailor 19
Skylab 59
slavery 12, 18, 46
sleds 52–53
Soto, Hernando de 32
South America 24, 30–31, 48–49, 50, 51
South Pole 54–55, 65
Soviet Union 58
space exploration 58–59, 69
Spain 22–23, 24, 25, 30–33
Speke, John Hanning 46, 65, 67

Spice Islands 20, 24, 30, 71
spices 9, 10, 16, 17, 18, 24, 25
Stanley, Henry 46–47, 63, 64, 67
Strait of Magellan 24
Stuart, John 38, 67
Sturt, Captain Charles 38, 67
submersibles 60–61
surveying equipment 39, 44

T

Tahiti 35
Tanganyika, Lake 46, 47
Tasman, Abel 34, 63, 66
Tasmania (Van Diemen's Land) 39
telescopes 28, 54–55
Tenochtitlan 31
Timbuktu 19, 71
timepieces 34
Timgad 11
trade
    Arabs 18–19
    Egyptians 8–9
    Greeks and Romans 10–11
    New World 20–25
    North America 43
    Phoenicians 6–7
    Silk Road 16–17
    Vikings 12–13
treasure 13, 25, 32
tribal warriors 46, 47

UV

underwater exploration 60–61
United States 42–45, 58–59
Verrazano, Giovanni da 40
Vespucci, Amerigo 23, 64
Victoria, Lake 46
Vikings 12–13, 40, 64, 65, 66
Vittoria 24, 25, 71

WZ

Wagenaer, Lucas 23
Waldseemuller, Martin 23
Wallace, Alfred 48, 49
Warburton, Peter 38
weapons
    African 47
    conquistadors 30–31
    Inuit 40–41
    Polynesian 15
    Viking 13
Wentworth, William 38
West Indies 22, 23, 30
Wilkes, Charles 44
Wills, W. John 38, 63
Wright brothers 56
Zambezi River 47

Acknowledgments

Dorling Kindersley would like to thank: Caroline Roberts, Robert Baldwin and Peter Ince of the National Maritime Museum, Greenwich; Joe Cribb, Simon James, Rowena Loverance, Carole Mendelson, Ann Pearson, James Puttnam, Jonathan N. Tubb and Sheila Vainker of the British Museum; Anthony Wilson, Eryl Davies, Peter Fitzgerald and Doug Millard of the Science Museum; Sarah Posey of the Museum of Mankind; Oliver Crimmen, Mike Fitton and Roy Vickery of the Natural History Museum; the Royal Geographical Society; the Royal Botanical Gardens, Kew; the Peabody Museum of Salem, Mass.; the Bathseda Baptist Church Museum and the Gallery of Antique Costume and Textiles. Thomas Keenes, Christian Sévigny and Liz Sephton for design assistance; Claire Gillard, Bernadette Crowley and Celine Carez for editorial assistance; Jacquie Gulliver for her initial work on the book.
Index: Helen Peters.
Additional photography: Dave King, Colin Keates (pp. 50–53), Mark Sexton (pp. 26–27). Maps: Sallie Alane Reason
The publisher would also like to thank Peter Chrisp for his help on the paperback edition.

The publisher would like to thank the following for their kind permission to reproduce their photographs:
(Key: a=above, c=center, b=below, l=left, r=right, t=top)

The Art Archive: British Library 70bl. Barnaby's Picture Library: 25tr. Bridgeman Art Library London/New York: 18tl, 22br, 40tr; Academie des Sciences, Paris, France 66bl; Alecto Historical Editions/British Museum 64c; Bibliotheca Estense, Modena, Italy 71br; Bodleian Library, Oxford 40bl; British Library 64cla, 64–65; British Museum 41tc; Hudson Bay Company 41bl; Metropolitan Museum of Art, New York 66tr; Private Collection 71cl; Royal Geographical Society 42tl, 42cl; Victoria & Albert Museum: 45bl, 62tr; Yale Center for British Art, Paul Mellon Collection, USA 68cra; Brierley Hill Glass Museum, Dudley: 48cr; Scott Polar Research Institute, Cambridge: 53c. British Museum, London: 9c. Corbis: Leonard de Selva 66br; Macduff Everton 69tl; Peter Turnley 67br. Dorling Kindersley: Space and Rocket Center, Alabama 59l. Endeavour Trust: Steve Wenban 68bl. Mary Evans Picture Library: 6tl, 8tr, 10tl, 17tr, 19tr, 19cr, 24tr, 26tr, 27tr, 28tr, 29c, 38tl, 38tr, 38cr, 40cr, 42tr, 49c, 50cr, 55br, 56tr, 56br, 58tr, 60tl, 60br, 64tr, 67cl. Getty Images: Hugh Sitton 68–69; Margarette Mead 65cl. Robert Harding Picture Library: 2br, lltr, 14bc, 15bl, 18c, 21tc, 21tr, 22cr, 27br, 30cl, 30–1, 35cr, 45c, 45cr, 46cl, 47tr, 47bl, 48bl, 50tr, 51tl, 57tr, 59tr, 62bc. © Michael Holford: 6br, 7c, 70br. Hulton-Deutsch: 12tl, 17cl, 20tl, 39tr, 56c, 58cl. Mansell Collection: 14tl, 21bl, 34cr. Museu de Marinha, Lisbon: 20br. NASA: 69bl, Dryden Flight Research Center (NASA-DFRC) /

NASA Image eXchange Collection 57br, JPL-Caltech 59br, STS-114 Crew / ISS Expedition 11 Crew 59cr NMAH/SI/Kim Nielsen 45br; NMNH/SI/Chip Clark 44tl. National Maritime Museum, London: 34br, 34tl, 35bl, 40d, 66–67. The Natural History Museum, London: 69ca. Nature Picture Library: David Shale 61br / L&M Dickinson 65tr. Peter Newark's Pictures: 43tr, 44br, 44cl. By kind permission of the Trustees of the Parham Estate: 34bl. Peabody Museum of Salem, Mass. / Mark Sexton: 26c, 26bl, 26–7c / Harvard University, Photo Hillcl Burger 44–5. Planet Earth Pictures/ Flip Schulke: 61c, 61bc / Brian Coope: 61bc. Popperfoto: 54tl, 55tc/ Royal Geographical Society: Ranulph Fiennes 67tc; 71 tr. Science Photo Library: 59tr. Syndication International: Front jacket bl, 2bl /Library of Congress, Washington DC 10bl/ Nasjonal-galleriet, Oslo 12bl, 16tl/ Bibliotheque Nationale, Paris 17bl/ British Museum, London 20bl, 23tc, 24cl, 24bc, 30tl, 30bl /National Maritime Museum, London, 34br, 40cl / National Gallery of Art, Washington DC 43bl/ Missouri Historical Society 45tr, 46tr, 46bc, 49bc/ John Hancock Mutual Life Assurance Co Boston, Mass. 52bl, 63tl. Werner Forman Archive: 64bl. Every effort has been made to trace the copyright holders and we apologise in advance for any unintentional omissions. We would be pleased to insert the appropriate acknowledgment in any subsequent edition of this publication.

Jacket: Front: Dorling Kindersley: The Darwin Collection, The Home of Charles Darwin, Down House (English Heritage) cla, National Maritime Museum, London c, tl, Royal Geographical Society, London tr, fcla; Back: Dorling Kindersley: The Trustees of the British Museum tl, National Maritime Museum, London cr, tr, cl, Natural History Museum, London fbl, Science Museum, London crb; Robert Harding Picture Library: bl

Wallchart: akg-images: IAM / World History Archive fcl; Alamy Images: The Art Gallery Collection fcrb; (map), ftl; Corbis: Stapleton Collection fcla/ (Vasco da Gama); Dorling Kindersley: National Maritime Museum, Greenwich, London cl, National Maritime Museum, Greenwich, London bl, Exeter Maritime Museum, The National Maritime Museum, London Exeter Maritime Museum, The National Maritime Museum, London / National Maritime Museum, Greenwich, London cb, British Museum Images ftr, fcr, Museum of Mankind / British Museum cla, clb, National Maritime Museum, London fcra, fclb, bc, Robin Wigington, Arbour Antiques, Ltd., Stratford-upon-Avon cr, The Science Museum, London fbr, br; Getty Images: General Photographic Agency / Hulton Archive bl/ (Antarctic expedition); © Royal Geographical Society: cb/ (cap); Werner Forman Archive: tl

All other images © Dorling Kindersley.
For further information see: www.dkimages.com

72